The Writer as Social Seer

The
Writer
as
Social Seer

by Robert N. Wilson

THE UNIVERSITY OF NORTH CAROLINA PRESS
CHAPEL HILL

© 1979 The University of North Carolina Press
All rights reserved
Manufactured in the United States of America
ISBN 0-8078-1363-X
Library of Congress Catalog Card Number 79-455

Library of Congress Cataloging in Publication Data

Wilson, Robert Neal, 1924–
   The writer as social seer.

   Bibliography: p.
   Includes index.
   1. Literature, Modern—20th century—History and criticism.
2. Literature and society. I. Title.
PN771.W57   809'.04   79-455
ISBN 0-8078-1363-X

For Joan and Tom

Contents

Acknowledgments

Henry A. Murray first encouraged my interest in trying to effect a rapprochement between the humanities and the social sciences, to merge the identities of sociologist, psychologist, and critic; he has been through many years a devoted friend, patron, and teacher. Malcolm Cowley and the late Conrad Aiken were influential as exemplars and tutors. In sociology, Leo Lowenthal, Hans Speier, and César Graña have shown the way to me and to any others audacious enough to essay a content analysis of literary works. Among literary critics, Ian Watt and William Barrett have been kind respondents as well as models.

My close friends and colleagues, Lloyd Rogler, Harold Wilensky, Ralph Patrick, and Patricia Rieker have consistently supported these efforts. In particular, Berton H. Kaplan has read and commented perceptively on the entire manuscript. Finally, my students at Harvard, Yale, and The University of North Carolina at Chapel Hill have been lively and willing partners in a series of dialogues for course credit called "Literature and Society."

My thanks to Rosalie Radcliffe for her patient, effective work in preparing the manuscript.

The author is grateful to the following publishers and authors for permission to reprint excerpts from the works listed below:

THE ANTIOCH REVIEW: Robert N. Wilson, "Fitzgerald as Icarus," vol. 17, no. 4, December 1957, ©1957.

THE ATLANTIC MONTHLY: Svetlana Alliluyeva, "To Boris Leonidovich Pasternak," ©1967 by Copex Establishment.

AVC, INC.: Robert N. Wilson, The Study of Lives, ©1963.

BEACON PRESS: Lionel Trilling, Freud and the Crisis of our Culture, ©1955. Reprinted by permission of Diana Trilling, Executor of the Estate of Lionel Trilling.

DAEDALUS: Clifford Geertz, "Deep Play: Notes on the Balinese Cockfight," ©1972. Reprinted by permission of Daedalus, Journal of the American Academy of Arts and Sciences, Boston, Massachusetts. Winter 1972, Myth, Symbol, and Culture.

DELL PUBLISHING CO.: James Baldwin, Another Country, ©1963, and Go Tell It on the Mountain, ©1965.

DODD, MEAD AND CO.: George Bernard Shaw, Selected Prose of Bernard Shaw, ©1952. Reprinted by permission of The Society of Authors on Behalf of the Bernard Shaw Estate.

DOUBLEDAY & COMPANY, INC.: Martin Esslin, The Theatre of the Absurd, ©1961, 1968, 1969 by Martin Esslin.

DUKE UNIVERSITY PRESS: Milton C. Albrecht, "Psychological Motives in the Fiction of Julian Green," Journal of Personality, March 1948, ©1948.

FARRAR, STRAUS & GIROUX, INC.: Walker Percy, The Message in the Bottle, ©1954, 1956, 1957, 1958, 1959, 1961, 1967, 1972, 1975 by Walker Percy. Daniel Schneider, The Psychoanalyst and the Artist, ©1950. Reprinted by permission of Daniel Schneider.

GROVE PRESS, INC.: Samuel Beckett, Endgame, ©1958, and Waiting for Godot, ©1954.

HARCOURT BRACE JOVANOVICH, INC.: Richard Wilbur, Advice to a Prophet and Other Poems, ©1960 by Richard Wilbur.

HOUGHTON MIFFLIN COMPANY: Arthur Mizener, The Far Side of Paradise, ©1965 by Arthur Mizener.

THE JOURNAL OF AESTHETICS AND ART CRITICISM: Robert N. Wilson, "Literature, Society, and Personality," vol. 10, no. 4, ©1952.

THE JOURNAL OF SOCIAL ISSUES: Robert N. Wilson, "Samuel Beckett: The Social Psychology of Emptiness," vol. 20, no. 1, ©1964.

MACMILLAN PUBLISHING CO., INC.: Robert K. Merton, Social Theory and Social Structure, ©1957 by Free Press. Georg Simmel, The Sociology of Georg Simmel, tr. and ed. by Kurt H. Wolff, ©1950 by Free Press. Martha Wolfenstein and N. Leites, Movies: A Psychological Study, ©1950 by Free Press. Reprinted by permission of Macmillan Publishing Co., Inc.

WILLIAM MORROW AND CO.: Margaret Mead, Male and Female, ©1949.

RANDOM HOUSE, INC.–ALFRED A. KNOPF, INC.: Albert Camus, The Myth of Sisyphus and Other Essays, ©1967; The Plague, ©1958; The Rebel, ©1956; and The Stranger, ©1959. Czeslaw Milosz, The Captive Mind, ©1953. Boris Pasternak, Doctor Zhivago, ©1958. Ivan Turgenev, Fathers and Sons, ©1950.

RUSSELL & RUSSELL: Leon Trotsky, Literature and Revolution [1925], ©1957.

MIT PRESS: Hans Speier, Social Order and the Risks of War, ©1952.

CHARLES SCRIBNER'S SONS: F. Scott Fitzgerald, The Great Gatsby, ©1925; The Last Tycoon, ©1941; The Stories of F. Scott Fitzgerald, ©1951; and This Side of Paradise, ©1920. Zelda Fitzgerald, Save Me the Waltz, ©1932. Ernest Hemingway, A Farewell to Arms, ©1929; For Whom the Bell Tolls, ©1940; In Our Time, ©1925; and The Sun Also Rises, ©1926. Andrew Turnbull, ed. Scott Fitzgerald: Letters to His Daughter, ©1963.

THE VIKING PRESS: Malcolm Cowley, A Second Flowering, ©1973 by Malcolm Cowley. All rights reserved. Reprinted by permission of Viking Penguin, Inc. Arthur Miller, Death of a Salesman, ©1949, 1977 by Arthur Miller. All rights reserved. Reprinted by permission of Viking Penguin, Inc.

Introduction

Elizabeth and Tom Burns have paraphrased Frank Kermode to say that the job of the literary critic-sociologist is to make sense of the way imaginative writers make sense of our lives. These essays are an effort to do so, to discover the meanings several important modern novelists and dramatists have assigned to the human condition. My method is essentially a thematic analysis of literary works, and, to a much lesser extent, of creative behavior or the artist's social role. The works discussed are not in any strict sense "representative" of modern literature; they reflect rather my own values, inclinations and curiosities—but they are all, I think, of substantial literary, sociological, and moral significance. My primary concern has been to identify the critical issues, the persistent questions about human conduct, that inform certain literary creations of the twentieth century.

A close reading of the "texts" of a culture may be expected to yield some knowledge that is not so readily available from other sources of inquiry. In literature, this contention has been well illustrated by Leo Lowenthal's provocative study *Literature and the Image of Man*. One of the firmest assertions of the value of sophisticated content analysis in the social sciences is that of Clifford Geertz.

The culture of a people is an ensemble of texts, themselves ensembles, which the anthropologist strains to read over the shoulders of those to whom they properly belong. There are enormous difficulties in such an enterprise, methodological pitfalls to make a Freudian quake, and some moral perplexities as well. Nor is it the only way that symbolic forms can be sociologically handled. Functionalism lives, and so does psychologism. But to regard such forms as "saying something," and saying it to somebody, is at least to open up the possibility of an analysis which attends to their substance rather than to reductive formulas professing to account for them.[1]

The application of sociological and psychological perspectives to the arts is a perilous and much-debated enterprise. I have chosen, from among the many possible approaches, to keep the literary work itself in the foreground of attention. Therefore, the conceptual apparatus and the data of the social sciences form only the background of these essays; their presence is rather more implicit than explicit. One of the recurrent, if often too bluntly construed, issues in the study of literature occurs between those critics who would emphasize giving exclusive attention to the "internal" properties of the work of art (*explication du texte*) and those who wish, for a variety of reasons, to set literature in the context of the social history that nurtures it and the psychological contours of the writer's life. I have tried here to step gingerly between these extremes. My view toward literature and its relation to the social and psychological environment has been very wisely expressed by Archibald MacLeish.

This myth of the poetic imagination which students in colleges are called on to admire as literature has become a myth of myself which I—student, teacher, man, woman, whoever—am called on to live as life. And one sees how this miracle has been accomplished. It has been accomplished not by squeezing the pips of the text but by a perception which has one foot in the text and the other in the world so that the two, text and world, are made to march together. . . . I think "English" always stands with a foot in the text and a foot in the world, and that what it undertakes to teach is neither the one nor the other but the relation between them. The greatest poem, removed from the ground of our being, is an irrelevance. The ground of our being without the poem is a desert. "English," I think, is the teaching which attempts to minister between.[2]

In the following essays, "social science" is "the teaching which attempts to minister between."

I shall focus here on the individual Walker Percy calls "the novelist of ultimate concern." Such writers ask radical questions about the nature of man and about his role in the social and physical universe he inhabits.

The idea that art may have some predictive value is rooted in several theoretical traditions. Essentially, one must assume that a reading of the expressive symbol systems of a culture can reveal important things about that culture. In the sociology of literature this assumption has a long history, going back at least to Taine and Mme. de Staël, and is usually phrased as some version of the proposition that literature "reflects" society. I shall not here belabor the obvious conundrums concerning the mode of reflection, the aspects of a society that are most and least effectively reflected, the problem of sampling, and so on. Another, related assumption, but one not crucial to my argument, is that art not only mirrors what is going on but also has a potential influence on society. Audiences attending to expressive forms may find their perceptions and behaviors altered as a consequence of this aesthetic involvement. In literary critical theory it is often asserted that art contributes to changes in our language; therefore, in the long run, it inevitably changes us because it changes the linguistic mold in which we perceive and report on the world. In sociological theory, notably in Weber, Sorokin, Mead, and Parsons, there is widespread acceptance of the idea that expressive symbols both indicate the values of a society and, in turn, shape its concepts of self and other and of communication.

Setting aside the issue of literature's influence on behavior, we may look at two facets of art's usefulness as an indicator of what is happening or what is likely to happen. The philosopher William Barrett claims flatly, "The forms of imagination that any epoch produces are an ultimate datum on what that epoch is."[3] He proceeds, in his remarkable study of modern literature *Time of Need* to go quite far in backing that claim. For our study we have only to accept that the artist is a very sensitive antenna whose perceptions are faithful to what is going on around him. The other facet concerns the ancient image of the artist as prophet. Most sophisticated observers, including artists themselves, tend to argue that the artist does not actually foresee the future in straightforward terms; rather he is so exquisitely attuned to the present that he appears to be in certain ways ahead of his times. He perceives what is already here, but he does so more rapidly and alertly than the nonartist. Thus the poet Conrad Aiken wrote that the artist is the only true contemporary. Walker Percy puts this theme vividly: "The novelist is less like a prophet than he is like the canary that coal miners used to take down into the shaft to test the air. When the canary gets unhappy, utters plaintive cries and collapses, it may be time for the miners to think things over."[4]

What, then, might a close reading of modern literature suggest about our future? I shall essay a sketch of central themes drawn from eight writers: Fitzgerald, Hemingway, O'Neill, Miller, James Baldwin, Camus, Pasternak, and Beckett. They are all canaries, and probably we miners should think things over as we slip into the last decades of this century.

Chapel Hill, N.C.   Robert N. Wilson
January 1979

The Writer as Social Seer

1

Literature, Society, and Personality

In the order of thought, in art, the glory, the eternal honor, is that charlatanism shall find no entrance; herein lies the inviolableness of that noble portion of man's being.

St. Beuve

Anna Sergeyevna was silent for a little. "And so you haven't the least artistic feeling?" she observed, putting her elbow on the table, and by that very action bringing her face nearer to Bazarov. "How can you get on without it?" "Why, what should I need it for, may I ask?" "Well, at least to enable you to study and understand men."

Turgenev, *Fathers and Sons*

The relations between literature and life have long been a matter of debate among writers, critics, and other students of society. Extreme positions have ranged from the view that literature is the highest, most intense expression of human activity, embracing the most important issues, generating and reflecting all that is vital in the intellectual and moral world, to the contrary claim that novels and poems are merely entertaining ornaments which have no solid connection with the mundane universe of operating social and economic forces. But these may be readily seen as false alternatives, distracting our attention from the central task of exploring the various relationships that may exist between the arts as characteristically human enterprises and the

3

diverse other facets of behavior. Neither the acts of writing or reading nor the content of literary works themselves ever stands in a simple, direct connection with other areas of life. Literature is not a mirror or a psychoanalytic document, or a report on the state of the nation, although it may indeed contain elements of all these and more. A great book, or even a good book, is a vision of the author; yet it is no longer solely his, for the writing and sharing have endowed it with a kind of independence, a content in and of itself.

Avoiding, then, the temptation to reduce literature to some easily scored instrument in the social concert, we can question the interplay between arts, artist, audience, and the general fabric of life. The newer studies of man—the social sciences—have tended to neglect the arts. In part, this neglect is due precisely to the complexity of the interplay, the great difficulty of counting or measuring or validly assessing the role of creative and appreciative activity in the individual personality or the social pattern. Art blindness has resulted in a foreshortened model of the human being and a grey-toned, pedestrian portrait of society. The desire to simplify and reduce behavior to its minimum terms has led the psychologist and sociologist to attend almost exclusively to activities, such as child rearing or industrial organization, that seem somehow more tangible than the arts. Artistic creativity and aesthetic experience, those uniquely human and distinctively civilized concerns, have been shunted off as trivial and superficial.

The disregard and even pronounced animus shown by social scientists toward art is undoubtedly caused in some degree by their need to separate themselves from an "unscientific" humanist tradition. Only recently emancipated from philosophy and theology and proudly striving for a rational, empirical approach to social events, the student of man feels obliged to disavow the unsystematic perceptions of poet or playwright. Brusque manner and awkward expression are the outward signs of scientific respectability; the morning coat of the humanities must be renounced for the shirtsleeves of the laboratory physicist. Poetry, drama, the novel, no matter how brilliant their insights, have been judged to present no "true," verifiable statement of the human condition; nor have the making and receiving of artistic creations been credited with forceful implications for men's actions.

One may now detect certain changes in this attitude. The concern with language as a mold of human experience and as a vehicle of social intercourse is leading the student of behavior toward some commerce with poetry and literary criticism. The growing recognition of man as builder and inhabitant of a sophisticated symbolic environment is directing attention once more to the philosopher and artist. As undeniable facts of contemporary life, increased leisure and education are compelling us to look with renewed vigor at creation and recreation as distinctively human forms of serious play.

Literature as a Descriptive Technique and Source of Knowledge

In its broadest sense, literature may be viewed as a primary source of knowledge about man. Failure to recognize that humanity's central concerns have been most faithfully delineated over the centuries by painters, sculptors, and writers is equivalent to renunciation of any real effort to understand the species. Art is an attempt to communicate images, sensations, or ideas from one man to other men and as such can scarcely avoid being of the essence of human intercourse. It is thus inherently valid as a source of information and suggestion for the student of man. That most pronounced talent of homo sapiens, the ability to conceive of himself and his environment as separable objects of attention, implies that self-searching is the very basis of artistic expression. It is a truism that most first novels are autobiographical; succeeding ones are too, although commonly in lesser degree because the author's widening experience mutes the personal strain. Whence else the insight so vital to creative activity and convincing communication? Introspection is the clue to the first indisputable value of art as a technique of the social studies. All who analyze human behavior would affirm the proposition that the individual's unique view of life, his own definition of the situation in which he finds himself, is indispensable to the understanding of man singly or men in groups. Artists have obviously provided us with the richest mine of material in existence for the study of self-perception.

Psychology, especially in those aspects committed to deep clinical assessment of the whole personality, is naturally the closest ally and most direct heir of literary techniques. The more aware among professional psychologists are quite prepared to admit that literary representations of character have a measure of coherence and a fullness of descriptive detail unapproached by the sketches of contemporary psychology. Novelists and poets must face different criteria than scientists in the evaluation of their work; they are not dependent on independent empirical verification of their hypotheses but rather on judgments of the degree to which their work approaches certain implicit models of stylistic grace and emotional exactitude. The reader, or at least sufficient numbers of readers, must testify that the author's work "rings true," but true or false the writer's statements are not susceptible to the kind of demonstration we expect in science. Thus literary character portrayals may be imprecise or even utterly wrong in terms of our best psychological knowledge. Yet it is certain that the writer conveys an internal symmetry of motives and a keen flavor of experience that are unattainable by science alone and are critical to full comprehension of personality.
Murray attests to the value of literary insight.

A future historian of social science may be surprised to find that, in writing case histories such as are published here, the psychologists of our time show no sign of having been influenced in any way by the twenty-five centuries of literature which have preceded them. The lines of derivation are quite different. Perhaps there is no enlightenment for a clinician in Aristotle, Lucian, Plutarch, Montaigne, Shakespeare, Bayle, Stendhal, Balzac, Dostoevski, Tolstoy, Nietzsche, Proust, and others of their stature; but my suspicion persists that the science of man would be carried forward more surely if those of us who undertook to unravel, interpret, and formulate the life histories of normal or abnormal personalities were familiar with the works of the great masters who, assuming that the understanding and portrayal of motives belonged to their special province, directed their acute intelligences to this office.[1]

This view is further elaborated by Gordon Allport. After noting the effect of the natural and social sciences on personality study, he contends that the humanities have been perhaps most powerful of all in their influence on psychology: "Throughout the ages, of course, this phenomenon of personal individuality has been depicted and explored by the humanities. The more aesthetic philosophers and the more philosophical artists have always made it their special province of interest." Allport sees certain specific ways in which the literary approach betters that of psychology, especially in charting the course of natural life history through time: "In literature, personality is never regarded, as it sometimes is in psychology, as a series of unrelated actions. Personality is not like a water-skate, darting hither and yon on the surface of a pond, with its several fugitive excursions having no relation to one another. Good literature never makes the mistake of confusing the personality of man with that of a water-skate. Psychology often does."[2]

Literature observes man as he moves through situations and knits the diverse facets of the personality into a consistent whole. Psychology can learn much from the artist about the analysis of character traits and the perception of lineaments in the vital subjective image of the self. This is not to deny that writers may make personality too coherent, as Dickens, for instance, so often does. Allport concludes that art may indeed be valuable in the study of man: "Personality is not a problem for science nor a problem for art exclusively, but for both together. Each approach has its merits, but both are needed for even an approximately complete study of the infinite richness of personality."[3]

If one accepts the proposition that the arts in general and literature in particular afford a useful entry into the study of personality, it is proper to ask about their further utility in understanding the social context of personality. What can the writer tell us about those patterns of interpersonal relations that constitute human society? Obviously, the habitual and accidental relations of man to man lie at the very heart of the novel as an art form. Dostoevski does more than present a brilliant picture of Raskolnikov's self-destruction; he also describes a place and time, a slice of Russian society, that teach us much about the social organization of nineteenth-century Russia. Similarly, The Magic Mountain explores the detailed style of relationships in a minute social compass that approaches a closed system; Anna Karenina treats important aspects of Russian social hierarchy as well as the problem of civilized adultery; and The Grapes of Wrath deals in part with the necessary arrangements of a viable, if small and transitory, group life. The inevitable distinctions of power and position in mass industrial society, now or in the future, are nowhere more strikingly set forth than in *Brave New World* or Orwell's *Animal Farm*. The artist, then, explains and describes "what life is like" in a variety of settings; in this endeavor, he conveys not only the elements of social intercourse, with an eye for significant detail, but also the mood or tone of the human circumstance. The social scientist may perhaps array details more economically, for some purposes, than the artist, but it is debatable whether his description ever communicates the feel of a social milieu as effectively as the work of the perceptive artistic observer.

Literature, then, is itself a prime repository of knowledge about human behavior. It can also find an exceedingly important place in the disciplines of psychology, sociology, and anthropology through its effectiveness as a medium of illustration. The concepts of science often impress students and the educated lay public as sterile and barren, remote from the colorful immediacy of life. When these concepts are clothed in literary examples, however, their relevance and explanatory power may be immeasurably better understood. Literature's scientific value is, of course, not merely that of vibrant illustration; often an artistic example prompts the scientist to revise his abstract model or teases him on to more subtle perceptions. Most of the great novels can be used to clarify aspects of sociological theory. Dickens, for instance, abounds in detailed accounts of the difficulties involved in working within, or with changing, the traditional institutions of society. Recall only the "miasma" of the law as sketched in the masterly beginning of *Bleak House*.

In the analysis of individual psychology, again, novelists and playwrights give us keen glimpses into the unfolding of motives and into the nuances of emotional conflict. Poets, above all, lay bare the human loneliness with the subtle, precise accents of the singer's response to a world he may or may not have made. It is perhaps not the sheer accident of a classical education that led Freud to draw on Greek tragedy for his illustrative symbols in the Oedipal theory or to contrive the term "lesbian" to denote a particular sexual inclination once known on the isle where Sappho cried. Instances of acute perception into psychodynamics are as numerous as great writers or profound books. From the Bible, the Platonic dialogues, and the ancient wise books of the Orient to the stories and plays of contemporary Western society, artists have marvelously represented the family drama, the themes of love and hate, and the search for a mature concord of desires.

Literature as an Expression of Society and Personality

Literature may be most broadly considered as an extant and vital part of man's culture, of his equipment for viewing the world and his place in it. Like most facets of culture, literature is enmeshed in the curiously circular pattern that underlies the stability of social arrangements. It is at once a product of human beings and an influence upon them. Just as in child development the parents' modes of behavior are learned by the young and in turn propagated, so in artistic activity the creations are received and to some extent reexpressed in the thoughts and lives of the audience. The arts reflect the individual minds and social environments from which they spring; but they also have a profound effect on the succeeding texture of that environment and on individual styles of life.

Because literature is always closely tied to a specific language, it is perhaps the most likely of all the arts to represent the unique features of the society in which it arises. Unlike painting or music, whose mediums are in a certain sense universal, writing is to a great extent inseparable from the particular culture of which it is an expression. As does language, literature mirrors the life of its times, although the correspondence is seldom direct or transparently valid. Even when the writer expresses themes or values quite different from those espoused by his compatriots, his rootedness in a common linguistic frame implies that he must refer his conceptions, however divergent, to the major premises of his age. Thus, if the writer is not upholding an old order or affirming a conventional perception, his new order or original perception is still dynamically related to the values it refutes or extends. Whether its mirror is the stark confrontation of the dressing-table or the distorting image of the amusement park, literature cannot avoid telling us something both important and true about its social surroundings.

In a variety of instances, literature makes important cultural elements explicit with a clarity unattainable by either the participants or more "objective" reporters. The artist's peculiar capacity for mixing empathic involvement with shrewd detachment lends him a unique perspective on the situations he describes. The growing pains of American social and intellectual independence from Europe, and especially from England, are surely nowhere better analyzed than in the novels of Henry James. *Piers Plowman* tells us much about a certain phase of European culture, not only because it portrays a way of life, but because it was in fact a product of that way of life. Although the arts can provide the student of society with an invaluable description of the details embodied in a style of life—dress, manners, speech forms, and so on—they are perhaps most vital in their communication of the general feeling tone of a culture, of the implicit assumptions of value and attitude that underlie the surface flow. Literature is a paramount source of insight for the scientist who attempts to formulate the core values of a culture, to characterize its guiding tenets in brief compass.

If one of our pressing needs is, as it seems to be, a more thorough understanding of the major features of American life, it is foolhardy to neglect American literature. Emerson, Thoreau, Melville, Henry James and Henry Adams, the "Genteel Tradition," the poets and novelists of the 1920s, the Depression, and our own postwar era—all of these, surely, are central to such an enterprise. An example from another culture might be seen in the way one's sense of Japanese values, as analyzed by Ruth Benedict in *The Chrysanthemum and the Sword*, is enriched by the study of Lady Murasaki's tenth-century *Tale of Genjii*.

The sociologist may draw on the arts for subtle and subjective interpretations of the gross systematic relations that are his chief concern. Family structure, the hierarchical ordering of society, the patterned activities of a community—these may not be fully comprehended without a close look at what they mean to the persons involved. Literature deals with precisely this question of the meaning of social forms as they are perceived through the individual's lens. Fielding's description of eighteenth-century English gentry is more than amusement; no squire ever acted like Squire Western, yet we acquire from *Tom Jones* a flavor that helps us to understand English society of that period. Such data are, to be sure, a part of English history, but they are also directly pertinent to the present shape of English life. Contemporary Britain is, in some sense, influenced by country courtyards that knew the tilt of a stirrup cup or the obeisance of a groom. The nature poetry of a Shelley or Wordsworth is very certainly relevant to the rurban complexion of modern Britain.

Students of society have made the analysis of the "prerequisites" or invariant features of a social system one of their main tasks. Nowhere have these central characteristics of human organization been more spiritedly treated than in the vast utopian literature. From More in his *Utopia*, to Bellamy, in *Looking Backward*, idealistic writers have tried to depict more or less "perfect" systems; from them we gain not only a notion of what has seemed logically desirable to observers at a given time but also a vivid account of the implications of social rearrangements for personal life. Although social amelioration is not the first aim of the scientist, his thinking must be informed by a knowledge of where societal strains are most acute. Here the literature that is popularly termed "sociological" comes into play. For the literature of social protest is more than the fantasies of malcontents; it may be a true index of tensions, and such tensions may first be made apparent by the sensitive artistic perceiver. The artist's vision may presage change. From *Uncle Tom's Cabin* and the plays of Gorki to the Farrells and Steinbecks, the artist as reformer has both represented strain and been himself a symbol of it. He has sometimes helped speed a radical change in administrative or legal policy and hence in society. The Bazarov of *Fathers and Sons* anticipated, perhaps, a portion of that spirit in nineteenth-century Russia that was to culminate in the Soviet experiment.

If literature reflects the society of which its author is a member, it also represents the chief elements in the personalities shaped by a particular social context. Obviously there is no single "typical" mode of psychological makeup that can stand for all the varieties of personality found in a complicated civilization. There are, however, recurrent major themes in individual functioning characteristic of most members of a defined social group. The relatively common features of personality engendered by the child-training patterns and reinforced by the main values

of a society have often been most strikingly expressed in literature. We thus find clues in the novel, drama, or poem that
indicate something about individual character as well as social
environment. The youth of classic Russian novels were rarely
happy people; one may speculate that national conditions under
the Czars were such as to promote, as one element in the
personalities of youthful intellectuals, a feeling of frustration and
aimlessness. Again, the poetry of Michael Wigglesworth or the
religious dicta of Cotton Mather could not fail to impress one
that the overpowering sense of sin preached by the Puritan
theocracy was woven closely into the personalities of early New
Englanders. Victorian enthusiasm, optimism, and moral rigor are
well depicted in the great English novels of the age; Dickens,
Thackeray, Trollope, diverse as they may be, do exhibit in their
fiction many of the principal elements of personality in their
society. The psychological props of colonialism in the "high
noon of Empire" can scarcely be discussed without frequent
reference to Kipling's poems.

The author's own personality may of course be interestingly
explored through his work, although there are two significant
dangers in this effort. The first danger is that the investigator,
forgetting the complexity of artistic creation and the writer's
ability to assume many guises, may propose a deceptively simple
one-to-one correspondence between man and book. The second
is that the analyst may see the writer's personality as wholly
typical and representative of his nation or social class milieu,
whereas artists with their special gifts and special responsibilities
are extremely unlikely to be themselves characteristic products
of their environment. A perceptive recent exercise in psychological analysis is Erikson's study of George Bernard Shaw through
an examination of his autobiographical writings. Rosenzweig
has offered a brilliant essay on Henry James's personality. Albrecht justifies his concern with fiction as a source of insight into
motivation: "This study suggests in general that literary works
like other manifestations of human behavior fall into definite
patterns consistent with the essential nature of the author; that
underlying such truisms as 'fiction reflects the personality of the
writer' are systems of interrelated and complex meanings largely
untouched by aesthetic principles and literary classifications;

that autobiographies and memoirs, though often misleading in statement and interpretation, can yield to significant psychological and sociological investigation."[4]

Literature as an Influence on Society and Personality

One of Oscar Wilde's more thoughtful aphorisms is, "Nature imitates Art more than Art imitates Nature." This is a brilliant overstatement of the truth that human nature, at least, may be importantly affected by artistic experience. Personalities and societies may owe certain facets of their development to the influence of literary works. The individual artist, especially in literature, is of course molded to some extent by the efforts of his predecessors. But on the broader scene of general human development, literature may also be viewed as a primary source of models, of values and attitudes that condition both individual growth and the content of social institutions. Certainly we recognize the influence of literature on the lifelines of outstanding persons in a variety of professions and environments. Autobiographies point again and again to the remembered effect of a great poem or novel; it is probably just to assume that the Battle of Waterloo was won in the classrooms of Eton, where schoolboys had been for generations steeped in the literature of leadership. One may object that only a tiny fraction of any population is exposed to literature with enough intensity to produce a lasting imprint, but this neglects both the peculiar force exercised on their societies by the best-educated minorities and the remarkable phenomenon of "percolation"—the imitation of the talented by those less gifted and the rehearsal of important themes in inferior, derivative artistic products.

A society's common values are reinforced, and sometimes revised, through the medium of art. If the writer restates the accepted values of a group, and does so in an appealing, convincing fashion, his work shores up the existing system. It may confirm the members of the society in their traditional ways of behaving. The steady churchgoer finds support for endless Sunday mornings on a hard pew if he is assured by the novelist that such is indeed the pattern of the elect. An elderly spinster may find that her honor was in fact worth saving if some Victorian heroine wins the world by retaining wholesome virginity. It is noteworthy that the Communist countries have put so much emphasis on the ideological tenor that is expected of their literary figures in the belief that what the writer says is critical to maintaining totalitarian order. Soviet and satellite leaders evidently feel that the arts are central to social life and deserving of the time and energy required to monitor them.

Although it is more difficult to adduce instances of social change that are intimately related to artistic influences, the literature of social protest does have some impact. There are perhaps two quite different ways in which imaginative works shake the organization of society. The first is direct and restricted; it may be exemplified by the supposed impact of Upton Sinclair's *The Jungle* on the regulation of the American meat-packing industry. Beyond this kind of immediate dramatization, so popular in the "proletarian" novel of the 1920s, lies another, more profound conception of the arts as agent of social change. Here the artist does not call attention to some disorder in the surface forms of contemporary life but rather presents us with a new way of seeing and valuing. If the new perception is accurate and the language is adequate to express it, the work may be woven deeply into the unfolding texture of society. Santayana's *Three Philosophical Poets* shows how, each in his own manner, Lucretius, Dante, and Goethe effected perceptual transformations in European culture. In a less grand but more readily demonstrable sense, the dramas of Ibsen and Shaw may be related to changed concepts of law, responsibility, and sexual roles. According to the popular tradition, the door Nora slams in *A Doll's House* was heard all over Europe; even if it was heard by only a few there seems little doubt that Ibsen stimulated fresh thoughts on marital concord.

Literary experience is seldom considered to be an important factor in the individual's life history. We correctly search first for the interpersonal events, especially the events of early childhood, that Freud and others have shown to be critical in character development. Yet modern man lives in a world of words, a world where his almost every act must be related to a symbolic, linguistic environment. In emphasizing face-to-face encounters, we often overlook the more subtle relation between writer and reader via the printed page. Reading, however, is as surely a part of experience as any other; far from being a substitute for "real life," it is immersed in real life.

Literature affects the individual perhaps most keenly in the development of the positive, forward-reaching regions of the self. It helps to set goals of life-style and character attainment that may be summed up as the ego ideal, or ideal of self. The maturing individual is known by modern psychology to be capable of change, of directed pursuit of values commensurate with adult life; it is just these sophisticated, often highly conscious shifts in posture that seem most susceptible to literary influence. Artistic experience, says Allport, may seriously determine the path of intellectual and emotional development: "However entered, if it is entered at all, the world of ideas is a factor that shapes the more complex reaches of personality, and not infrequently it is the most important factor of all."[5]

Examples of literary revelation and inspiration are legion. One might mention Heywood Broun's statement that the reading of *Looking Backward* turned him toward socialism, or the report that China's Mao Tse-tung greatly admired "heroic" novels at an early age. Literature, because one of its prime goals is character portrayal, naturally abounds in descriptions of social roles. Not only may the reader gain from artistic representations a conception of what is required in his relations with others, what his reactions should be to the actions of other people in their roles, but he may be stimulated in the choice and definition of those of his own roles that are more or less self-determined. An individual does not choose the role of son or daughter, but he does to some extent select the role of father or friend, lover or lawyer. In the former instances, he may model his behavior along lines suggested by fictional characters; in the latter, both desire for the role and patterns through which it is realized may be based in part on literary example. The ego ideal, the individual's subjective portrait of the sort of person he would like to be, may in extreme cases be derived directly from some admired character in a novel or play. More often this ideal of self is a composite creation, a blend of favored exemplars in which fictional models are a large element. Allport says in *Personality*: "Every mature personality may be said to travel toward a port of destination, selected in advance, or to several related ports in succession, the

Ego-ideal always serving to hold the course in view."[6] The ports of this journey, and the means of travel, often owe much to the conscious or unconscious trying out of "parts" first encountered in literature.

Literature should, then, be regarded as a field in which the nature of man may be richly explored. It is at once a part of man's culture—his total fund of styles for living—and a detached commentary on that culture. Resulting from the individuals of a society, it indicates certain things about them and their forms of group behavior. Acting upon the reader, literary works are a shaping force in personality development and social organization. The arts and the artist are central, not peripheral, to any informed cognizance of human motives or actions.

2

F. Scott Fitzgerald

Personality and Culture

Fitzgerald was perhaps the last notable writer to affirm the Romantic fantasy, descended from the Renaissance, of personal ambition and heroism, of life committed to, or thrown away for, some ideal of self.

Lionel Trilling, *The Liberal Imagination*

The relation between the artist's personality and his work, while obviously intimate, can never be made wholly explicit. Creativity is too elusive, too fundamentally mysterious, to afford a point-by-point correspondence between the man and the art. Yet the artist's role has shifted historically on the question of the individual's degree of identification with his books or paintings or music. From the anonymous art of the Middle Ages, dedicated to the glory of God, one may trace a movement toward ever greater concern with the artist as a person, toward a highly individualized art dedicated to the glory of self. In some instances this tendency has resulted in a relative disregard of the work, in its overshadowing by the symbolic importance of the artist's person. Rimbaud, for example, has perhaps been more influential as the prototype of a role—the alienated, rebellious writer at odds with society—than as a poet to be read for his poetry.

As Trilling notes in the above passage, F. Scott Fitzgerald may stand as an exemplar of self-exploitation in the novel. His life and work were so interwoven that the distinction between them blurs: in a sense, he imagined and created his life and lived in his fictional protagonists. The quiet life of the conscientious artisan, the poet whom Milton counseled to drink plain water from a wooden bowl, was utterly foreign to Fitzgerald's conception of the writer's role. Rather, the author must live as his characters live, must make their style his and his theirs. In living up to a dream, an ideal of dramatic selfhood, Fitzgerald merged both his personality and the society in which he lived into his artistic representations. It would be as true to say that his life was a novel in progress—and like his last novel, unfinished—as that his novels are autobiographical. As Malcolm Cowley says, "Sometimes the heroes started as very different persons and were transformed imperceptibly, as he worked over them, into an image of the author."[1]

When he strove toward an ideal of self, a receding image of glorious and transcendent being, Fitzgerald expressed not only a personal disposition but a recurrent theme in American culture. In an exaggerated, pure form, he struck what many regard as the unique chord in our national experience—a wholehearted allegiance to an imagined future. This allegiance entails impatience with the present in all its imperfection and enjoins striving toward an as yet unrealized state of grace. With maturity, the individual commonly scales down his own American Dream to more modest proportions. He learns to tailor his goals, to limit the ideal, and to nourish his capacities for a more restricted achievement. Fitzgerald, however, was unusually tenacious, and his vision of the future was unusually full-blown. His desire encompassed the public life of the celebrity, the semiprivate life of a star in a select social firmament, and the solitude of the literary craftsman. His refusal or inability to compromise these alternative and perhaps mutually exclusive selves may lie at the root of his tragic unfulfillment. But that very disdain for discipline, that failure to conserve his personal resources, may also be germane to the marvelous zest that informs his best writing.

Fitzgerald and Icarus

If Fitzgerald's ideal self was marked by a catholicity so extreme as to thin out his talent in diffuse activities, it was at the same time distinguished by an intensity of literary aim. All that we know of his writing habits indicates a constant struggle to excel, to evoke precisely the right response from the reader by character and mood. His notebooks demonstrate how carefully, especially in his later period, he tried to create characters who would not make a psychologically false move. It seems likely, from the evidence of his last years in Hollywood and the incomplete fashioning of *The Last Tycoon*, that Fitzgerald might at length have muted the emphasis on himself as novelist extraordinary and devoted his life more thoroughly to art than had been the case. Nevertheless, his foreshortened career stands dedicated to an ideal of self so intense and so demanding that it invites comparison with the Icarian myth.

Henry A. Murray has described a psychological pattern that he terms the "Icarus complex."[2] This pattern is an induction from a single intensive clinical history, although it is corroborated by a wealth of psychological and literary evidence. Although Murray's elucidation of the complex is based on a variety of indices to his subject's personality, including projective tests, interviews, and observed behavior, Fitzgerald's life and work are so well documented that we are justified in seeking out a parallel configuration despite the lack of clinical knowledge in its strict sense. Fitzgerald, of course, does not conform to every facet of the Icarus complex; a scientifically isolated "type" never corresponds to any richly unique human being. Yet the psychologist is inevitably struck, in this instance, by an amazing correspondence between the themes exhibited in an exceedingly interesting male adolescent personality, studied clinically, and those exhibited in Fitzgerald's personality and the characters of his novels. These engaging parallels by no means reduce Fitzgerald to a clinical type; rather, they contribute to a coherent portrait of an extraordinarily talented writer.

The Icarus complex is distinguished by the following themes, most of which may be strikingly illustrated in the novelist: burning ambition and exhibitionism; desire to ascend to great heights; desire to be the center of all eyes; a precipitous fall; craving for immortality; depreciation and enthrallment of women. Obviously, the gifted and ambitious individuals of most societies exhibit some of these characteristics in some degree. The poet or philosopher may be peculiarly marked by them, according to Murray, and "for the fullest expression of the complex one must turn to ardent romantic poetry (Byron, Shelley), to mythic philosophy (Socrates in *Phaedrus* or Nietzsche in *Thus Spake Zarathustra*), or to some form of up-yearning (erotic) mysticism."[3] In significant literary and psychological respects, Fitzgerald may be viewed as a romantic poet.

Fitzgerald and his created figures abound in excess ambition. As Arthur Mizener observes, in *The Far Side of Paradise*, "As a small boy Fitzgerald lived, as he said later, 'with a great dream' and his object was always to realize that dream."[4] His sights were set very high, and they continued to be set on transcendent goals long after the usual fantasies of adolescence. Two remarks he made in his early days are significant: "If I couldn't be perfect I wouldn't be anything," and, in undergraduate zeal to Edmund Wilson, "I want to be one of the greatest writers who ever lived, don't you?" The idealized self is perhaps a conspicuous feature of any artist's or any man's self-picture. What makes it unusual in Fitzgerald is the height of his aspiration and his habit of comparing himself on a lifelong basis with the giants of literature. Mizener observes, "He was thirty before experience succeeded in convincing him that 'life was [not] something you dominated if you were any good.'"[5]

Exhibitionism and its complement, voyeurism, come through clearly. The endless parties of Scott and Zelda, their outrageous, funny, pathetic escapades, the final confession Fitzgerald wrote for *Esquire*—all contribute to the impression of a profound desire to exhibit, a desire not at all confined to the display of admirable qualities. It may well be that all writers are somewhat voyeuristic; their stock in trade is a propensity to peer into other worlds, other styles of life. Fitzgerald, however, in his unalloyed curiosity about the milieu of the rich (the curiosity displayed in his story "The Rich Boy" and embalmed in the famous exchange with Hemingway) showed extreme needs of this sort. As Malcolm Cowley noted of Fitzgerald in his Princeton days, he viewed Eastern university life and the parties of the wealthy as the urchin does the candy store, his nose pressed against the window to an exotic world.

All of Fitzgerald's heroes are ambitious, and all except Anthony Patch of *The Beautiful and Damned* are immoderately so. It should be remarked that their aspirations are not confined to a single path, for instance, to a vocation, but embrace many facets of work, love, and informal social intercourse. The heroes are self-consciously playing roles and striving for effects. Their eyes are on the future, on the creation of a dramatic personality and an orbit in which the personality may most graciously move. The two earliest heroes, Amory Blaine and Anthony Patch, aspire without fulfill-ment, although their dreams are not lessened by lack of success. Of Amory Blaine, Fitzgerald says: "Always, after he was in bed, there were voices—indefinite, fading, enchanting—just outside his window, and before he fell asleep he would dream one of his favorite waking dreams, the one about becoming a great halfback or the one about the Japanese invasion, when he was rewarded by being made the youngest general in the world. It was always the becoming he dreamed of, never the being. This, too, was quite characteristic of Amory."[6]

The later, more mature figures back up their ambition with genuine ability, but it is still overwhelming in magnitude. Jay Gatsby, Dick Diver, and Monroe Stahr each dream of brilliant success. Diver and Stahr are transcendent individuals in psy-chiatry and movie production, respectively, but strive even higher. The mysterious Gatsby is entirely transparent about his central concern, his dream of self.

The truth was that Jay Gatsby of West Egg, Long Island, sprang from his Platonic conception of himself. He was a Son of God, a phrase which, if it means anything, means just that—and he must be about his Father's business, the service of a vast, vulgar, and meretricious beauty. So he invented just the sort of Jay Gatsby that a seventeen-year-old boy would be likely to invent, and to this conception he was faithful to the end. . . .

And as I sat there brooding on the old, unknown world, I thought of Gatsby's wonder when he first picked out the green light at the end of Daisy's dock. He had come a long way to this blue lawn, and his dream must have seemed so close that he could hardly fail to grasp it. He did not know that it was already behind him, somewhere back in that vast obscurity beyond the city, where the dark fields of the republic rolled on under the night.

Gatsby believed in the green light, the orgiastic future that year by year recedes before us. It eludes us then, but that's no matter—tomorrow we will run faster, stretch out our arms farther. . . . And one fine morning—[7]

It is perhaps symptomatic that *The Great Gatsby* is generally acknowledged to be Fitzgerald's finest novel and one of the truly distinguished American works of the twentieth century. In addition to its marvelously taut form and precise language, *The Great Gatsby* epitomizes the mystery and glamour of the future dream; without question, the struggle to fulfill a lofty unrealized conception of self is prominent in American values and central to Fitzgerald's psychic economy.

The desire to rise, leap, fly, and be tall among men is obviously akin to the zealous ambition that characterizes Fitzgerald and his characters. It is astonishing to find how often and how vividly images of flight occur in the novels. Indeed, *The Last Tycoon* is explicitly built around the transcontinental flights of its hero, Monroe Stahr, between Hollywood and New York, and Fitzgerald's notes show that flight was to have been an even more important theme in the unfinished portion. Fitzgerald appears as a literal Icarus in a curious description written by his wife Zelda in her avowedly autobiographical novel *Save Me the Waltz*: "There seemed to be some heavenly support beneath his shoulder blades that lifted his feet from the ground, as if he secretly enjoyed the ability to fly but was walking as a compromise to convention."[8] In his notes for *The Last Tycoon*, these images occur under the heading "Airplane Trip": "My blue dream of being in a basket like a kite held by a rope against the wind. . . . It's fun to stretch and see the blue heavens spreading once more, spreading azure thighs for adventure."[9] The sexual symbolism of the latter is interestingly in keeping with the fantasies of the individual from whom the Icarus complex was originally derived; that young man dreamed of flying through the air on a maid's rump.

Probably the most coherent single expression of the ascension theme and Icarian imagery is found in the discussion of Monroe Stahr, the incredibly gifted Hollywood producer of *The Last Tycoon*.

"What I wanted to know," he told me ruefully, "is how he ever got to be Mr. Stahr."

I'm afraid Mr. Stahr could never have answered that one; for the embryo is not equipped with a memory. But I could answer a little. He had flown up very high to see, on strong wings, when he was young.

And while he was up there, he had looked on all the kingdoms, with the kind of eyes that can stare straight into the sun. Beating his wings tenaciously—finally frantically—and keeping on beating them, he had stayed up there longer than most of us, and then, remembering all he had seen from his great height of how things were, he had settled gradually to earth.[10]

Murray's next component is "a craving for unsolicited attention and admiration, a desire to attract and enchant all eyes, like a star in the firmament."[11] Fitzgerald and his heroes display a keen appetite for this kind of adulation. The social worlds of the novels revolve around the heroes' persons, not simply because the stories are told from their various perspectives, but because they are in fact at the center of their respective universes.

From the start, Fitzgerald experienced the overwhelming admiration of others; for his mother, and later for teenage companions, he was an admirable figure, glorying in the role of cynosure. Arthur Mizener speaks of "his mother's undiscriminating admiration." Fitzgerald himself later said, "I didn't know till fifteen that there was anyone in the world except me." In the days of frantic partying, when, in Zelda's familiar remark, "it was always tea-time or late at night," the Fitzgeralds stood in the center of a circle. One feels they never cared to stand anywhere else. It was as if they said, "Come, look, marvel at how we can be at once so witty and talented, so gay and handsome." The thirst for recognition, as writer and as person, may be related to the constant entertaining that helped insure a state of perpetual insolvency for an author whose novels and short stories were almost uniformly successful.

Brilliant and exciting gatherings of people, of the *best* people, invariably center on the magnetism of such protagonists as Gatsby, Dick Diver, and Monroe Stahr. The invited and uninvited guests of Gatsby's great house parties were perhaps as much in search of a legend as of free liquor; his very mystery and lack of identity served to focus a myth of distant, awe-inspiring personality. In one of the most intriguing passages of *Tender Is the Night*, the girl Rosemary sees Dr. Richard Diver as symbol and center of a company so gay and rich and diverting that the world seems to balance at his dinner table. Any other setting, any other party, is cosmically irrelevant. But their élan is not a group achievement; it is created and controlled by Dick Diver and his wife, Nicole. An ephemeral thing, this grace and spiritual plenitude rests in Dick's hands, so that its continued existence depends upon his ability to maintain a somewhat euphoric mastery.

A variation of the theme is observed in *The Last Tycoon*. Here Stahr, although he is not the partying type, makes a dramatic entrance into a crowded club. At once all action stops, except the action of watching Stahr and whispering—as lesser figures do throughout the book—about his character and supposed motivations. Like all Fitzgerald heroes, Stahr asks a great deal of life; the notes for the novel make this clear, and the words here emphasized might serve as a motif for the heroes as for their creator: "Back to the main theme: Stahr cannot bring himself to marry Thalia (in the novel *Kathleen*). It simply doesn't seem part of his life. He doesn't realize that she has become necessary to him. Previously his name has been associated with this or that well-known actress or society personality, and Thalia is poor, unfortunate, and tagged with a middle-class exterior that doesn't fit in with *the grandeur Stahr demands of life.*"[12]

Murray, finally, has recapitulated the blending of psychological elements that characterizes Icarus before his fall: "Already we begin to see a close, emotionally logical—indeed, an almost inevitable—connection, if not fusion, between ascensionism and cynosural narcism: the way to attract all eyes is to be very tall, to stand erect above the multitude, and best of all to rise in the air like a god."[13]

Having attained a certain height, in most cases towering dominance, the hero falls as Icarus fell when the sun had melted his waxen wings. Of the five novels, only one concludes with the hero at or near the position he had held when the story opened. Amory Blaine, in *This Side of Paradise*, has lost romantic illusions but retains his youth and a life to come. Dick Diver (*Tender Is the Night*) lives on, but is socially dead, corrupt, isolated from the mainstream of his profession and from his friends, and divorced from his beloved Nicole. Anthony Patch (*The Beautiful and Damned*) sails with his psychosis toward an unknown port. The remaining two, Gatsby and Stahr, meet violent deaths: Gatsby is shot, and Stahr, exemplifying Icarus, was to have died in an airplane crash at the end of *The Last Tycoon*.

Fitzgerald seems to say that the gaudy dream—and the dreams are vital, for "the handle by which he took hold of his characters was their dreams."[17]— is at length unrealizable, or, if realized, unsatisfying. It is, nevertheless, difficult to imagine any of these men as "settling down," as striking any kind of compromise with their aspirations, or as living uneventful and undistinguished lives. They are exciting to author and reader only while they are on top of the world and larger than life. Perhaps, then, Fitzgerald is also saying that the game is worth the candle and that one should have few regrets even if the descent from the heights is precipitous.

The life Fitzgerald lived, as well as the ones he wrote, hewed starkly to the Icarian theme. He went far up in popularity to become the poet of the Jazz Age and far up in critical esteem as the author of *The Great Gatsby*. His books brought wealth, fame, and a dramatic life-style. He won the wife he sought, the Southern beauty who had once (before publication of *This Side of Paradise* and overnight success) seemed beyond his reach. Parties, travel, friendships with men and women of literary and social distinction—all these fell to him easily and quickly. Descent from such heights of self-realization could only be brought about by a cruel convergence of inner and outer circumstance.

The Fitzgeralds overspent to maintain the houses and clothes and parties that meant so much to both; saddled with debt and constant financial anxiety, the novelist was forced to interrupt his plans for major works and to concentrate on producing saleable short stories. *Tender Is the Night*, the effort of several years, failed to sell, although it is now recognized as one of his most exciting and sensitive novels; the popular explanation for this failure is that it deals with the personal problems of the wealthy and talented, a theme poorly calculated to interest Americans in the Depression year of 1933. Alcoholism began to interfere with his writing and living. Perhaps most telling of reversals, the beautiful Zelda developed a psychosis that required hospitalization and destroyed family life. And so Fitzgerald fell to the depth in which he wrote that he now knew the dark night of the soul as described by St. John of the Cross, "where it is always three o'clock in the morning."

If Fitzgerald thus suffered the same fall from grandeur that he had charted for his heroes, it is most important to stress that his own story does not end at the nadir. Rather, he was able to come back part-way toward artistic excellence if not toward the resumption of his total dramatic social role. The heart attack that foreshortened *The Last Tycoon* is believed by many critics to have interrupted his finest novel as well as ended a stubborn struggle for artistic rebirth and the revival of personal integrity.

The craving for immortality may be taken as intrinsic to the writer's role; in Herbert Read's phrase, he yearns for "a paper eternity." It is not strange, then, that Fitzgerald wanted his books to last. However, his heroes, none of them artists if one excepts the tentative longings of Amory Blaine and Anthony Patch, also strive for an immortality of a different variety, a type well described by Murray. "If resurrection (re-ascension) is not to be vouchsafed a man, there is the possibility of *replication*, which may be defined as the process whereby one or more persons are transformed in the image of the subject. It is the complement of identification, or emulation: the implanting of a memorable and impelling image of the self in the minds of others."[15]

To imprint others with the seal of self, as a ring cuts an image in soft wax, is a prominent aim of Fitzgerald's chief characters. Thus the whole theme of *The Great Gatsby* could be seen as Jay Gatsby's unforgettable impress of his self-conception on the mind and spirit of the narrator, Carraway. As Carraway says of this fascination: "I wanted no more riotous excursions with privileged glimpses into the human heart. Only Gatsby, the man who gives his name to this book, was exempt from my reaction— Gatsby, who represented everything for which I have an unaffected scorn. If personality is an unbroken series of successful gestures, then there was something gorgeous about him, some heightened sensitivity to the promises of life, as if he were related to one of those intricate machines that register earthquakes ten thousand miles away."[16] So Dick Diver, too, lives on in the minds of those who surrounded him as an epitome of social grace. The last hero, Monroe Stahr, was to find his immortality by exerting a very powerful and specific influence following the plane crash that caused his death. Fitzgerald's notes tell us that Stahr's briefcase would be found in the wreckage by a small boy and that its contents would then inspire the boy to follow an honorable, outstanding career.

Depreciation and enthrallment of women, a conception of them "as objects to be used for narcistic gains," is the one component of the Icarus complex for which the evidence in Fitzgerald is scant and often contradictory. It is true that the women his heroes marry or hope to marry are always, except in *The Last Tycoon*, creatures of unusual beauty and remoteness whose social status is high; thus marriage to one of them is a self-enhancing achievement that gratifies the hero's wish to be admired and envied. It is also true that in no case is a stable, lasting relationship achieved. An exceedingly narcistic view of women is given by Gatsby, on being told that the woman he desires really loves her husband, in his remark, "In any case, it's only personal." That is, the personal concerns of another are inconsequential in the light of Gatsby's cosmic self. Finally, there is little doubt that Fitzgerald's own marriage to Zelda, the Southern patrician, represented both a triumphant achievement and a reward for his success with *This Side of Paradise*.

But depreciation is surely not a prominent feature of these relationships. Rather, the women of Fitzgerald are adored in a wholehearted way, in a rather quaint, old-fashioned mood of romantic chivalry. One feels his attitude toward them never advanced in some respects far beyond the worshipful gaze of the Ivy League undergraduate, circa 1920, toward the prettiest girl at the ball. This adoring stance also deepens and becomes enriched through the devotion lavished on the ill wife, on Nicole by Dick Diver and on Zelda by Fitzgerald. One is forced to conclude, then, that while women indeed fed the self-exaltation of the hero, they were also valued for themselves. As part of the dream and partners in reality, Fitzgerald's women secure a central place; they focus some of the most tender and moving passages in the novels.

The life and novels of Fitzgerald may thus be said to represent a sequence of themes characteristic of the clinical syndrome termed the "Icarus complex." This personality style overreaches and founders on the insatiable quality of magnificent dreams, of idealized images. To analyze the progression of psychological elements is to see the writer more clearly, but decidedly not "to explain away" or undercut his creative achievement.

One must, of course, beware of pushing an analogy too far; despite their similarities, the college student who modeled the Icarian career and Fitzgerald are quite different individuals. Fitzgerald was a successful writer and attained a very hard-won maturity, whereas the young man on whom the Icarus complex is based had not yet achieved his vocation or outgrown an adolescent attitude toward sex.

In striving for transcendent success, Fitzgerald accomplished much. A less noble conception of self might have produced less noble works of the imagination. Although he called himself "an indifferent caretaker of my talent," the astonishing fact is that, given the half-world of life with Zelda, life with alcohol, life with a party in the making or made, he sustained a creative thrust that affords us his small but fastidious artistic legacy.

Fitzgerald as Cultural Exemplar

A literary work, its creator's personality, and the cultural framework within which the work is written and read are always implicated in a network of relationships that forms the province of the sociology of literature. Although one may choose to emphasize a special aspect of this network, as in studies of creative personality or readership, the relationships are best seen as reciprocal and mutually enriching. A worthy social scientific approach to art should at once tell us something about the artistic object and something about human behavior, so that literary and behavioral analyses are both enhanced. Here I shall focus on Fitzgerald and his novels as exemplars of certain major patterns in American life and propose that, although Fitzgerald is most often known as "the poet of the Jazz Age," he has a wider relevance than as a social historian of the 1920s.

If the novelist portrays social life and moves us with his descriptive gift that evokes the essence of things seen and felt, he also is an analyst. The perceptive novelist never merely describes at random, nor does he enunciate pure fantasy. Rather, he abstracts from the flow of experience and distinguishes significant elements of intrapsychic and interpersonal life. Like a scientist, a creative writer tries to make sense of the raw stuff of experience. But the writer employs different techniques, perhaps notably a rich—not parochial—and precise language, and he has a different end in view. The artist tries to convince others of his truths through immediate apprehension of the felt rightness of what he says; in contrast, the scientist uses logical demonstration or experimental replication to gain assent. Despite all their precious and inerasable distinctions one from the other, there is an ultimate sense in which artist and scientist are alike in saying to the audience, "This is the way it is." The novelist is not an inexact sociologist. In most cases, and decidedly in Fitzgerald's, he is an intelligent man striving for entire precision in his report on the social universe.

Why should we, as students of American life, refer to Scott Fitzgerald, quite apart from whatever aesthetic sensibility we may feel toward his extraordinarily fluent style? Art may do at least three things for the social scientist: illumine, confirm, and stimulate. Impressing known ideas upon us by its power of endowing them with dramatic life, the novel illumines and illustrates what we think we know about our society. It confirms our findings, in however singular a manner, by bringing us to realize that one very sensitive observer has remarked things we have also noted in our more pedestrian approaches. Finally, art stimulates by affording us fresh insights and ideas; we take these all the time from one another, from our own tradition and schol arly literature, because none of us can do firsthand research in more than a fragment of the social field. Why should we not then draw upon the record of a gifted researcher into the human situation, a novelist who thought long and experienced strenuously, who then reported what seemed to him the crucial features of American life?

Fitzgerald was very much a part of the life of his times. His representativeness of and immersion in the culture around him are shown both by his contemporary popularity (he was one of the few artists who gained both substantial literary esteem and a great deal of money from his work) and by his desire to live fully, often to his detriment as artist, in that decade and generation whose twin sobriquets of "roaring" and "lost" he so well earned. In addition to the glory and gray aftermath of a transient fame, he had staying power; his skill of craft, his aesthetic and humane talents, assured him of a good bit more than passing merit. If he is in the long run remembered as a minor novelist—and he will surely be remembered—the term "minor" will properly refer to his slender output rather than to flaws in the few novels he gave us. It may well be that some think Fitzgerald is dated just because he had such a fine ear for the speech and a fine eye for the artifacts of the twenties. I should maintain on the contrary that American character and culture are plumbed in his art for a much longer run. Gatsby's motorcar and clothes and mansion may give way to the sports cars and split-levels of another day, but Jay Gatsby the dreamer is as true to 1978 as to 1925.

The way in which Fitzgerald's novels, and to a lesser extent his life, will be employed here is cogently argued by Wolfenstein and Leites: "The common day-dreams of a culture are in part the sources, in part the product of its popular myth, stories, plays, and films. Where these productions gain the sympathetic response of a wide audience, it is likely that their producers have tapped within themselves the reservoir of common day-dreams. Corresponding day-dreams, imperfectly formed and only partially conscious, are evoked in the audience and given more definite shape."[17] As an ordering scheme for the relation of the literary vehicles to prominent American values, I shall hew fairly closely to the "value orientations" identified by Florence Kluckhohn.[18] No analytical system is able to apprehend fully the range and subtleties of cultural pluralism in an advanced industrial society, but these have the immense merit of combining general relevance to a host of philosophical essentials with specific linkage to behavior. The resonance of Fitzgerald's art for the American temper may be explained in part by the intimacy of his themes with certain dominant values. The degree of fidelity to core American dispositions raises problems in literature as in life, and Fitzgerald's excursions from the conventional pattern are often as interesting and revealing as his customary pursuit of the main goals down the main path. Let us see how the novels and the man adhere to the classic description of American belief and action.

Future Time

The tyranny of tomorrow is so frequently remarked as a feature of middle-class life that American orientation toward the future is quite often taken for granted and seldom questioned or analyzed. It may be said to have two major aspects, which are unequally stressed by Fitzgerald. The more mundane element, and the less important in the novels, is the habit of rational planning toward ends whose accomplishment rests on deferred gratifications, training, saving, the husbanding of the self and its resources for an explicit later fulfillment. This is the world of thrift and Poor Richard, of correspondence courses and the down payment on the cottage. It is a world too compulsive and tawdry for most of Fitzgerald's heroes, who want to run faster and more gracefully; his people are also more often of the upper-middle class, whereas the strict pattern of large renunciations and minor rewards seems more typically a lower-middle-class phenomenon. Nevertheless his gaudiest central figure was at length found to have rehearsed his sense of the future in just such a manner: after Gatsby's death his pitiful father arrives on the rich Long Island scene with a notebook which contains the adolescent Gatsby's schedule of self-improvement, a near caricature of the vulgar Protestant Ethic in its concern with habit training, hourly self-surveillance, and the last lovely admonition, "study needed inventions." It is significant that the more cautious and controlled facets of the future vision are so seldom seen in Fitzgerald's life or work. The missing pieces, the steps from dream to execution, are a clue to his and his heroes' failures, as they are also a clue to the grandeur of the dream itself.

Dreams are, of course, the second aspect of Americans' concern with the future. The deep desire to be and to experience that which is not yet informs our collective history of frontier and nationhood as it informs our personal histories of striving for the emergent self. Fitzgerald's men are imbued with a doctrine of personal manifest destiny. Perhaps here, in his great capacity to represent transcendent images of a future situation and a future self in believable and poignant terms, is the crux of Fitzgerald's continued appeal and relevance. The novelist and his protagonists overreach, their visions founder on a fundamentally insatiable quality, but in the process they show us the tone and tragedy of our marriage to the future.

Gatsby's green light may serve as a symbol of the future dream, with the added overtone of the traffic metaphor, which presses us to "go," to pursue the future with an exuberant energy. Margaret Mead has briefly and keenly evoked the theme of the unrealizable but demanding dream: "By the very nature of the dream none can attain it, and each particular household falls short of the ideal. Each house lacks some detail that is included in the house which no one lives in. No mother can be all that an American mother should be, no romance have all the qualities that true love should show. And this, not because the ideal is so high, but because it is a dream of the future rather than an attempt to reproduce the past."[19]

The hero of The Beautiful and Damned, Anthony Patch, is made to live the entire novel in anxious anticipation of a heritage that would be enriching and enabling, only to fall before an insanity that debased his unearned wealth. Here Fitzgerald is highly realistic, implying that the dream alone is not enough if it is unmatched by talent and vigor. Fitzgerald himself, of course, was a willing hostage to his dream of a future as a great novelist; he sought literary recognition, fame, and wealth. But he had the equipment to make the dream effective; for if he harbored visions of a unique personal grandeur, he also worked hard and perceptively at the novelist's craft.

Fitzgerald's chronology was not, however, exclusively attuned to the postponement of desire. Two of his most mature and fascinating heroes, the psychiatrist Dick Diver and the Hollywood producer Monroe Stahr, lived primarily in and for the present. And Fitzgerald, too, wished to live the dream right away, sacrificing his novels to the saleable short stories that afforded an instant cash return and the facilities for parties, travel, and a gaudy style of life. His lust for the present moment is related to the artist's need for sensory immediacy and to his intense drive for excellence and esteem in the form of quick reward. It should finally be remarked that Fitzgerald had the artist's respect for a tradition: if he exemplified the American stance toward an imagined future, he also lived with the insistent voice of a literary past, with the aesthetic conscience embodied in a Goethe or a Keats.

Individualism

Fitzgerald viewed the self as object and instrument; his goal was a particular image of selfhood, and his means was an exhaustive use of all that was in him. An individualistic version of human relationships is perhaps inseparable from the condition of being an artist in contemporary Western civilization. Fitzgerald lived his own life without much regard for collateral or lineal ties to others; moreover, his novels consist, at bottom, of heroic odysseys, of unfoldings of one person in the world that person shapes. It is a premise of the novels, as it is a premise of American culture, that unique individual destiny is the matter of first importance. Our attention is always centered on the hero's progress and personality; his lineage and his ties to others are significant only as they affect his rise in the world or as they reveal some aspect of his psychological makeup. Over the best of the novels there hangs an air of mystery, and this mystery is always focused on the hero: who he really is, where he comes from, what makes him run, where may he run to. Gatsby's acquaintances (he never had friends) search for the key to his motives and status; Dr. Richard Diver's secret is as much himself and his destiny as it is his wife's psychosis; Monroe Stahr in his mastery of film production requires explaining: "What I wanted to know—is how he ever got to be Mr. Stahr."

At heart, a very great deal of Fitzgerald's work is concerned with that most individualistic of problems, the struggle of a young man to make his way in a love affair, a profession, or a select social milieu. Success and money provided for Fitzgerald and his heroes a validation of self, but the validation required constant reinforcement in terms of social esteem. The concern is ever for the way the hero appears in his own and others' eyes. The heavy accent on the individual linked with the future dream and the belief in perfectibility makes Fitzgerald, in one sense, a much more sophisticated and artistically worthy Horatio Alger, Jr., as well as a genuine successor to the romantic novelists such as Stendhal or the young Goethe.

Human Perfectibility

The American axiom that human nature is a thing to be cultivated, if not entirely redesigned, in a search for a more effective, coherent, and better-behaved personality is central in Fitzgerald's art. Each hero is intent on making himself fit to hold high position in the affairs of men and the affections of women. Part of the dream about the future is, of course, the picture of oneself as he will then be. Gatsby's self-improvement is the prototype of that conscious molding through which one may be, and perhaps more important may appear to be, in controlled mastery of the situation of action. Dick Diver is drawn as a man striving for physical perfection (hardening his body on "the flying rings at New Haven"), for intellectual discipline in his profession, for social distinction in his Riviera circle. Diver tries, moreover, to mold his ill wife, Nicole, and perfect her sanity. Monroe Stahr wants to become so alert and perceptive that he can direct a great artistic and business enterprise down to the tiniest detail.

It should be emphasized that Fitzgerald did not postulate a benign or even a blandly neutral model of human nature. He embraced, rather, a strict code of self-control and gentlemanly inhibition that implied that the evil or mixed nature inherent in man must be disciplined if the characterological outcome is to be admirable. Some part of the fascination that the world of the rich and wellborn held for him was undoubtedly related to what he perceived as the aristocratic talent for self-control, for rounding the rough edges of passion and egotism. Fitzgerald had no illusion that men are any better than they should be; his stories repeatedly describe the outrageous behavior and moral decay of the man who lets himself go, who does not keep polishing his shield of honorable selfhood. Recall Tom and Daisy Buchanan of *The Great Gatsby*, who smashed things and then retreated behind their wall of money.

The novelist applied the doctrine of perfectibility to himself, and it was the belief in deliberate self-improvement that made his own dissipation and failures so hard to bear. Fitzgerald's dark night of the soul was the darker for being partly of his own devising. His notebooks and the letters to his daughter show how strenuously he tried to become a fine writer; self-exhortation is matched by the gently hortatory flavor of the letters to Scotty, in which he poured forth heart, head, and artistic conscience. Despite the generous evidence in his novels and life that he conceived of personality as a flexible and improvable process, there always lies within the conviction of guilt and sin and root evil. His Irishness and his art alike led him to think of himself as a "spoiled priest," spoiled perhaps by pride and alcohol. Fitzgerald's concept of human perfectibility—and personal responsibility for the posture at length assumed—is nowhere better illustrated than in his remark that he had been "an indifferent caretaker of my talent."

Mastery of Nature

Blending well with the theme of mastery of self is that of dominion over the natural world. Man's command of nature appears in Fitzgerald only by implication, as his is an urban, personality-centered universe, far from the pastoral dream. Nevertheless, it is clear that to the novelist human desire is the great lever, that the individual's elaborate and energetic control of himself and other men is paralleled by his control of the dumb cosmos. Like a frontier American, Monroe Stahr drives for the gap in the mountain range, and this metaphor is used to stress his talent for decisive choice. A ready control of all kinds of resources is associated with the upper-class style of life, which so obsessed Fitzgerald; one need instance only the extravagant fantasy of his short story "The Diamond as Big as the Ritz" to demonstrate how surely the novelist captured the characteristic American drive to subject nature to human whim.

Doing and Becoming

The last of five key American values to be discussed here, that of active, persistent external effort to cope with problems of whatever variety, is probably least clear-cut in Fitzgerald. Certain of his protagonists are undeniably "doers," Monroe Stahr of The Last Tycoon serving as perhaps the best example. And Fitzgerald in his exacting work as artist was the doer incarnate, the laborer in language. Most of the heroes, however, and the author much of the time, devoted themselves rather to a quest for personal symmetry and interpersonal grace. They chose the alternate path termed "being-in-becoming," which emphasizes a rounded internal development and the pursuit of a thoroughly civilized style of life.

One might say that the author and his heroes are too much concerned with beauty, the beauty of objects as well as of a mannered and measured social intercourse, to follow precisely the American route of busyness and brusque efficacy. Again it is important to remark Fitzgerald's fondness for, and partial identification with, the upper class, for it is just in this class that one finds the national passion for activity shading off into a heightened concern with graceful living and humane breadth of personality.

Fitzgerald thus exemplifies certain primary themes in American culture, as much in his life as in his created social universe. Seldom has a writer been so exquisitely attuned to the main currents of his own place and time and yet so sensitive to the deeper patterns that endure through the history of a society. If Fitzgerald is representative of cultural themes, able to supply evidence and insight about characteristic American postures, this very representativeness may rest on his unusual capacity for simultaneously living in his culture and writing of it. In him we find the keenness of a detached observer wedded to the passion and spirited involvement of a participant. Of those novelists with whom he might most obviously be compared—the adventurous Hemingway, the reclusive Faulkner, the journalistic, crusading Sinclair Lewis—Fitzgerald came closest to being absorbed in his culture, bound to its governing aspirations, and anchored in the kinds of concerns many of his nonliterary fellows shared.

Social Class

It is perhaps this thoroughgoing identification with the common dreams and anxieties of his milieu that makes Fitzgerald such an acute student of social differences. His acknowledged eye for telling details of language, dress, gesture, or decoration was related to his intense interest in the way Americans rank and evaluate one another. And that interest is, moreover, inseparable from Fitzgerald's own social position with its ambiguities of status and its perplexities about the process of rising or falling. Fitzgerald is exemplary in this aspect because he chose not to stand apart from the excited strivings and the habits of invidious comparison that marked his—and our—era. The status envy that he exhibited at Princeton and seemingly ever after, the desire to ascend into a rich and exotic layer of life, made him in some ways a classically marginal man, who responded swiftly to all the oscillations of a society on the move and on the make.

Lionel Trilling has observed that the traditional European novel has always pivoted on the facts of social differentiation: "If the English novel in its special concern with class does not . . . explore the deeper layers of personality, then the French novel in exploring these layers must start and end in class, and the Russian novel, exploring the ultimate possibilities of spirit, does the same—every situation in Dostoevski, no matter how spiritual, starts with a point of social pride and a certain number of rubles. The great novelists knew that manners indicate the largest intentions of men's souls as well as the smallest and they are perpetually concerned to catch the meaning of every dim implicit hint."[20]

The American novel has shared this obsession, of course, although the rapidity of change in class structure and the absence of fixed hereditary categories have perhaps made our writers less adept and less confident in dealing with class alignments. Henry James, Edith Wharton, and Theodore Dreiser are all distinguished in their perceptions of social difference and distance; today, however, they are too specialized or too remote in time to afford substantial insight into contemporary patterns. Sinclair Lewis and John Marquand describe a society we recognize, although Lewis's view of class strikes us as rather naïve and clumsy. Marquand's aesthetic qualifications are probably inferior to Fitzgerald's, but between them we can gain a good deal of knowledge about a particular range of the class structure—roughly the upper-middle class and the finer subdivisions of the upper class.

Fitzgerald nowhere tells us very much about status and its correlates in the social regions where most Americans live. He had no interest in the culture of poverty and slight interest in the workaday world of commerce and industry. What he does achieve is a remarkable perception of styles of life in the upper strata of the East and Midwest, and a fine sense of what these styles mean to the persons involved. The subjective impress, the psychological effect of holding a social position and striving to retain or enhance it, is delicately diagnosed. With his art, Fitzgerald enables us to enter the "little worlds" of class cultures and to experience the social-psychological significance of status.

Ernest Hemingway is usually assumed to have come off the winner in his discussion of class with Fitzgerald. When Fitzgerald claimed, "The very rich are different from you and me," and Hemingway replied, "Yes, they have more money," we at once think of the tough-minded Hemingway puncturing a misty romantic notion. Yet Fitzgerald may have been in some senses the more realistic of the two, emphasizing deep-going differences in style and seeing money as an index to separate social universes that cannot readily be bridged in terms of cash alone. Fitzgerald had perceived a social fact that most analysts of social class would verify: within broad limits the inhabitants of varied class levels live to themselves, immersed in a milieu of manner, value, and styled behavior that indeed makes the very rich "different from you and me."

There are many examples of this unusual sensitivity to social difference in his stories and in his life. Although Fitzgerald was early impressed with the peculiar glamour of the upper class and seemed as a Princeton undergraduate to have been naïvely susceptible to its alien charm, we find his maturing view to be in the true sense ambivalent. He was attracted and fascinated by a certain freedom, yet repelled by what he increasingly felt to be an enervating callousness: thus the reckless cruelty of the Buchanans in contrast to Gatsby's innocent yearnings, and thus "The Rich Boy": "Let me tell you about the very rich. They are different from you and me. They possess and enjoy early, and it does something to them, makes them soft where we are hard, and cynical where we are trustful, in a way that, unless you were born rich, it is very difficult to understand. They think, deep in their hearts, that they are better than we are because we had to discover the compensations and refuges of life for ourselves. Even when they enter deep into our world or sink below us, they still think that they are better than we are. They are different."[21]

Gatsby could never be at one with the Buchanans, could never penetrate their milieu, just as no one in "The Rich Boy" ever really shares Anson Hunter's ambience. When Fitzgerald dealt with the struggle for acceptance, the approach of a middle-class man to the environs of the rich, he sought and found the key detail. Dexter Green, the hero of "Winter Dreams," modulates his manner in shrewd recognition of the distinction between old and new money.

> Next evening while he waited for her to come down-stairs, Dexter peopled the soft deep summer room and the sun-porch that opened from it with the men who had already loved Judy Jones. He knew the sort of men they were—the men who when he first went to college had entered from the great prep schools with graceful clothes and the deep tan of healthy summers. He had seen that, in one sense, he was better than these men. He was newer and stronger. Yet in acknowledging to himself that he wished his children to be like them he was admitting that he was but the rough, strong stuff from which they eternally sprang.
>
> When the time had come for him to wear good clothes, he had known who were the best tailors in America, and the best tailors in America had made him the suit he wore this evening. He had acquired that particular reserve peculiar to his university, that set it off from other universities. He recognized the value to him of such a mannerism and he had adopted it; he knew that to be careless in dress and manner required more confidence than to be careful. But carelessness was for his children. His mother's name had been Krimslich. She was a Bohemian of the peasant class and she had talked broken English to the end of her days. Her son must keep to the set patterns.[22]

This was true too, in Fitzgerald's own striving. Although he wrote his way to upper-middle-class respectability and won the judge's beautiful daughter as his bride, he could only describe—not master—the assured way of life that characterized his friends the Gerald Murphys and others of secure upper-class position.

Another facet of his exemplary role may be seen in his rehearsal of the ancient American dialectic between East Coast and Middle West, cosmopolitan and provincial, sophistication and angular virtue. One feels that Nick Carraway, the voice of *The Great Gatsby*, speaks for Fitzgerald in his disillusion with the falseness of East Egg, Long Island, and in his determination to see the social world stand "at a kind of moral attention." The regional contrast is intimately bound up with the class contrast; the partly mythical égalité of the continental fastness is poised against the partly actual hierarchy of the effete East. In Fitzgerald there is a constant struggle between St. Paul, Minnesota, and the myriad settings of his adult career: Princeton, the Riviera, Long Island, Hollywood. In the classic vein, he remained the provincial young man even as he outwardly became a paragon of Manhattan worldliness. In a domestic version of Henry James's tension between wise Europe and young America, Fitzgerald was never quite certain of his regional and class identity; this very lack of sureness has, of course, been often remarked as typically American.

Fitzgerald tells us again and again that the attempt to breach class barriers is a perilous enterprise, requiring subtlety and courage. His heroes try, and they suffer. The gallant but untutored Gatsby, whose quest for status was presumably a mere adjunct to the winning of his dreamed Daisy, founders on the hard facts of social difference. Dick Diver of *Tender Is the Night* is much more than an upwardly mobile young professional; yet one of the things that shatters his promising psychiatric career is a noble desire to span two social worlds, the world of the very rich and the world of the dedicated vocational striver.

The novelist's own life was coated with that "foul dust [that] floated in the wake" of Gatsby's dreams. It was Fitzgerald's goal to live a style befitting the golden spokesman of a generation. He was by no means content to write a work of art; he had to live one, too, and his idea of the worthy literary career was inseparable from the rather heady style of one of his own protagonists. The remarkable merger of his identity with those of his heroes is baldly recounted: "Books are like brothers. I am an only child. Gatsby my imaginary eldest brother, Amory my younger, Anthony my worry, Dick my comparatively good brother, but all of them far from home. When I have the courage to put the old white light on the home of my heart, then . . . "[23]

When Fitzgerald had the courage, which was often enough to give him genius, he turned a blinding light on his heart's home. One of the things he saw there was the heavy penalty exacted by the social ascent. He pitted the iron demands of artistic craftsmanship against the lust for the externals of life, the perquisites of social status. But the latter, except perhaps in his last years, never seemed to him only externals. As for so many men in the United States, they constituted for Fitzgerald a validation of self, a tangible symbol of personal worth. Thus, we see his intermittent lapses from what he conceived to be his true literary vocation, his pursuit of the dollar through hastily written magazine short stories, his grinding indebtedness, and his last bondage to Hollywood while he squared accounts. Looking back, he thought the concern with a heightened life-style, the correlate of sustaining and enhancing social rank, was mistaken. And so he wrote to his daughter: "I wish now I'd *never* relaxed or looked back—but said at the end of *The Great Gatsby*: 'I've found my line—from now on this comes first. This is my immediate duty— without this I am nothing.'"[24]

Perhaps Fitzgerald's inability to escape the system of social class and to blunt his vulnerability to invidious comparisons of external status is ultimately revealing. If his personality structure was consonant with the Icarian theme, so much of his social behavior and his attitudes toward his society were consonant with major American values. If it would be an exaggeration to term the Icarus complex a characteristically American psychological type, we may at least affirm that there is something of Icarus—and something of Fitzgerald—at the very heart of our culture.

3

Ernest Hemingway
Competence and Character

Ernest Hemingway is in many ways the most whole and sound, and also perhaps the most truly contemporary, of the twentieth-century writers. Like Fitzgerald, he is entirely at one with his time and place, attuned to the specificities of modern life; but unlike his doomed friend and rival, Hemingway exhibits a mastery of self in the writer's role and a talent for the disciplines of sustained creative effort. His stoic persistence in his craft is perhaps inseparable from the reiterated image of heroic manhood in the novels themselves. Indeed, until the shattering end in madness and disability, Hemingway may be said to exemplify the artist as hero. Fierce, durable, he is essentially the poet struggling with all the ambiguities of language and experience, and thoroughly committed to his vocation. His justly famous lucidity, the spare and crystallized prose, is best seen as an act of poetic morality. Thus William Barrett rightly identifies the style as a first important clue to the writer's philosophy:

For him style was a moral act, a desperate struggle for moral probity amid the confusions of the world and the slippery complexities of one's own nature. To set things down simple and right is to hold a standard of rightness against a deceiving world. . . . Since the Greeks, language has been acknowledged as lying at the center of man's being. If style is what ultimately confers value on life, it is only within language that these values can find their ultimate expression. Style is not a literary confection, but a matter of balance, rhythm, and simplicity; and these are the qualities that hold a man together in his actions in the world. . . . For in language man comes to the truth of being that is both appropriate and possible for him.[1]

What are the values, the "truths of being," that Hemingway enunciates? And what may these tell us about the individual in today's social universe?

The novelist's style may be described as one of deceptive simplicity; that is, it is simple after the fashion of a good poem, with an apparently easy accuracy that is really hard-won. The immensely complex effort to set down the exact texture of the world as refracted through a very sensitive perceiver results at its best in a seemingly natural, effortless statement. Again like an achieved poem, Hemingway's prose strikes us as so quietly perfect that we cannot imagine the thing's being said any other way. His distaste for the abstract and the superfluous, his hunger for precision, is, as Barrett observes, "not a literary confection." Rather, the casual and unassuming but marvelously taut voice is designed to present us with the world of nature and man as directly experienced. The poet as namer is the most honest of living creatures, for he has no other purpose than to report on the world as it really is. Thus Hemingway's honesty, his telling us truly how things are, is at once the core of his style and of his philosophy.

The Solar Joy

Hemingway's first and last truths are remarkably akin to the dominant themes in Albert Camus and, from a quite different angle, to those in Boris Pasternak. These three so various novelists come together in celebration of a purified sensibility, an innocent love of being in the world. Cutting through grand phrases and empty syllables, they exalt in the plain confrontation of man with nature and with other men. Serge Doubrovsky, writing about Camus's reception in the United States, argues that American readers applaud the element of existential struggle and unremitting effort in his novels but often overlook the "solar joy."[2] So with Hemingway, we perhaps pay too much heed to the hero's battle, which is of unquestioned salience, and attend too little to his poetic joy, his sheer aliveness and sensual alertness. Hemingway sends us precise messages to, about, and through the senses; much in the manner of T. S. Eliot's "objective correlative," his writing makes us experience as his hero experiences and recreate for ourselves his being and "isness." We are told how things look, feel, taste, smell, sound. And never for a moment can we forget that the individual is a physical being in a physical universe. Existence for its own sweet sake, in a world of colors and textures, shadows and curves, is what we are enjoined to relish. The necessary but artificial fabric of values and concepts, vocations and ideals, is underlain always by the naked pleasure of sensory transactions. In the dense symbolic and institutional environment of modern society, we need to be reminded that we sweat and sleep, get rained and sunned on, feel shapes and see movements—and that our enjoyment of all these requires no justification, but does require recognition and praise.

Camus's tragic hero Sisyphus, who must be imagined happy in his endless task, is happy because he can feel the sun on his face and the rock under his hand. If Hemingway's protagonists are always losers ("winner take nothing"), as all men eventually must be, they are also always winners of something precious along the way. We shall see them winning the rewards of a certain exercised competence and a certain rectitude of character, but first things first. In the beginning and end they win the pleasures of being a live animal; this is by no means a mindless satisfaction, for it entails acute consciousness and time-binding memory in its realized savor. The glories of the senses are dearly bought, paid for in danger, disillusion, and the heavy pressure of responsibility for being a man.

Like Camus, Hemingway starts with the assumption that the lone individual faces an essentially meaningless universe, a world without plot or purpose except as man temporarily invents these for himself. In this world bereft of comforting illusions, the individual nevertheless has potent resources of cultivated skills and codified styles of life. In his moment-by-moment consciousness he is basically sustained by the sense of solar joy; involved with nature, friended by men and women, he need ask of this instant in time only what the instant willingly yields. To live is enough. Taking in naturally offered stimuli and reflecting upon them with one's full nervous organization is its own reward. From the earliest short stories through the major novels, Hemingway's heroes are never far from the touchstone of direct sensory experience; the experience is not always pleasant—pain is there as well as delight—but it is always compelling. And this being in the world attaches the person firmly to a natural order and imbues him with a sense of the intrinsic worthwhileness of experience. Life just is and has its own meaning right now, and long-run questions and answers may be healthily suspended. This is true for Nick Adams hiking and fishing and cooking up in Michigan, and it remains true to the end for Robert Jordan waiting for death on the pine needles or for the old man wrestling his fish. Here is Nick Adams in *Big Two-Hearted River*: "He walked along the road feeling the ache from the pull of the heavy pack. The road climbed steadily. It was hard work walking up-hill. His muscles ached and the day was hot, but Nick felt happy. He felt he had left everything behind, the need for thinking, the need to write, other needs. It was all back of him."[3] And Robert Jordan hangs on in pain to kill his last Spanish rebel in *For Whom the Bell Tolls*: "He was completely integrated now and he took a good long look at everything. Then he looked up at the sky. There were big white clouds in it. He touched the palm of his hand against the pine needles where he lay and he touched the bark of the pine trunk that he lay behind."[4]

The solar joy, with its undertone of fidelity to natural things and its strong current of unbidden delight, permeates Hemingway's first great success, *The Sun Also Rises*, and is, of course, implicit in the title. Wine drinking, trout fishing, eating and sleeping, being scrupulously attentive to the way things feel and smell, Jake Barnes exemplifies the man pleasured by the small increments that are a consequence of being alive. How apparent and somehow unremarkable it all seems. And yet, without the artist to remind us, how few men and women can really see and savor the daily round. The morality of Hemingway's prose, his capacity for finding a lyric in the ordinary rhythms of life, reminds one of James Joyce's remark about himself. Joyce confessed that he had the mind of a grocer's clerk, and it is just this simplicity, this thirst for the pedestrian, that is the authentic kernel of art.

Hemingway makes us *aware*, in exactly the way the critic Roger Fry describes:

The needs of our actual life are so imperative that the sense of vision becomes highly specialized in their service. With an admirable economy we learn to see only so much as is needful for our purposes; but this is in fact very little. . . . In actual life the normal person really only reads the labels as it were, on the objects around him and troubles no further. Almost all the things which are useful in any way put on more or less this cap of invisibility. It is only when an object exists in our lives for no other purpose than to be seen that we really look at it, as for instance at a China ornament or a precious stone, and towards such even the most normal person adopts to some extent the artistic attitude of pure vision abstracted from necessity.[5]

The great virtue of Hemingway's style is to remove the "cap of invisibility" from mundane experience. By persuading us that our every transaction with the world is rich with intrinsic meaning if we will only open ourselves to it, he reaffirms our humanity as sentient creatures, our psychological authenticity in a world we never made but are free to enjoy. His style is in some ways a matter of infinite caring, a vehicle of rectitude; in this sense the prose is the man. If we are to abjure the inexact and the sloppy in language, to strain for getting things clear and right, this discipline mirrors the way we should conduct ourselves as men.

The Responsibility of Being Human

Hemingway's code of behavior is not an easy one. It demands the intense alertness and commitment of the poet Conrad Aiden's credo: "to be as conscious as possible." The acute sensibility that lets a Hemingway hero enjoy the rain or the laughter or the wine is joined to a significant moral awareness. If the novelist's sense of solar joy, the unadorned valuing of experience as such, is the first element in such an awareness, what are other salient aspects?

Clearly Hemingway does not announce to us a code of behavior or standards of moral measurement in conventional terms. His criteria are usually implicit, to be inferred from his own or his protagonists' actions. Further, he refuses to credit the common currency of the language of morality; that language has become for him so abstract, so empty and abused, that it lacks any honest meaning. Thus Lt. Frederic Henry observes in *A Farewell to Arms*:

I was always embarrassed by the words sacred, glorious, and sacrifice and the expression in vain. We had heard them, sometimes standing in the rain almost out of earshot, so that only the shouted words came through, and had read them, on proclamations that were slapped up by billposters over other proclamations, now for a long time, and I had seen nothing sacred, and the things that were glorious had no glory and the sacrifices were like the stockyards at Chicago if nothing were done with the meat except to bury it. There were many words that you could not stand to hear and finally only the names of places had dignity. Certain numbers were the same way and certain dates and these with the names of the places were all you could say and have them mean anything. Abstract words such as glory, honor, courage, or hallow were obscene beside the concrete names of villages, the numbers of roads, the names of rivers, the numbers of regiments and the dates.[6]

Moral awareness is not geared to a received scale of evaluation in terms of altruism, religious belief, or fashionable communal norms. The bases of responsibility are composed more nearly of a certain kind of manliness, loyalty, and vocational fidelity.

Many critics have analyzed Hemingway's model of masculinity and have tended to see in it a blind, compulsive, over-reaching quality—a sort of mindless, if Anglicized, machismo. All genitals and guts and heart, no intellect. Yet the insistence on sensitive perception, a courageous style, and a stoic acceptance of the world as it is does not seem to spring from any failure of comprehension. Instead, it results from a disciplined simplicity, an austere concentration on some few rudiments of possible action in a testing situation. The individual in Hemingway's world does not ruminate on ultimate moral precepts but asks, rather, how to conduct himself in the here and now. The answer is to proceed with a certain style and to test oneself recurrently against the hard lines of experience. His first full-length hero, Jake Barnes in *The Sun Also Rises*, strikes this posture of existential acceptance, of learning by living, that is to persist throughout the fiction: "You paid some way for everything that was any good. . . . Perhaps as you went along you did learn something. I did not care what it was all about. All I wanted to know was how to live in it. Maybe if you found out how to live in it you learned from that what it was all about."[7]

Hemingway's conception of humanity lays a heavy responsibility upon the lone individual: to have the courage to live well and accept the world as offered—and not to whine about one's predicament. At bottom, the heroes share a mood of noble resignation and acceptance. Jake Barnes, Frederic Henry, Robert Jordan—each is a competent man, facing his own wounds and an ill-designed universe with dignity. Their fatalism expresses itself almost casually, in what the actor would term throwaway lines, but it is no less important for being muted. Jake Barnes again: "There was much wine, an ignored tension, and a feeling of things coming that you could not prevent happening."[8]

To be a man means to be tested and, indeed, to seek testing situations as a voluntary act of will. The crucibles appear in many forms, conspicuously including challenges to physical courage, but they seem always to involve ideas of loyalty. An individual keeps the secular faith at whatever expense; he is loyal to a conception of himself, to a friend or lover, to a shared vision of the desirable in human conduct: thus the loyalty of Frederic Henry to Catherine Barkley, of Jake Barnes to Brett Ashley, of Robert Jordan to Loyalists and comrades at arms and a treasured Spanish culture. Hemingway is one of the few American writers to deal at all adequately with friendship as a modality of human relations. Other novelists are better in treating of love, of the interior depths of the person, or of manners. But Hemingway is quite unusual in his capacity for catching the delight friends find in one another, in the small incidents of eating and drinking and joking together, in the mutual recognition that fosters intuitive understanding of the other and undergirds the elisions that mark friendly discourse—those necessary omissions that set friendship apart from more self-conscious, tutored interaction with its demand for the explicit and deliberate.

If one must be highly serious about being a man and being loyal, he must be serious as well about his vocation. The respect with which Hemingway regards a man's work is of course bound up with the novelist's own reverence for his craft, which I shall discuss more fully below. Again and again, whether the protagonist is a soldier, a bullfighter, a fisherman, or a writer, we find great weight given to his doing a task well. There is much in Hemingway of what someone has called "the religion of competence"; it is, perhaps in part, a substitute for more traditional forms of adherence to the sacred. One does a job, whatever it may be, with as much skill, grace, and endurance as he can muster. The line begins with Nick Adams fishing skillfully in Michigan streams and might be said to end with the old man towing his huge skeleton into safe harbor. In between, we have the young bullfighter, Pedro Romero, in *The Sun Also Rises*, who gains praise for his clean, direct line of attack; Lt. Henry, who rows through the long night to Switzerland and safety; Robert Jordan, who masters the politics of extremism and who sets his explosives with exquisite care.

And at the end, the Hemingway hero must also die well, as if the very end of life were one more opportunity to perform with competence. The famous definition of courage as "grace under pressure" is really an instance of the novelist's exaltation of competence. He says to us, "Whatever you do, do your damndest," for in the doing is the only redemption. He is at one with Shakespeare's dictum that "we owe God a death," but he has also the fortitude toward dying expressed in *Julius Ceasar*.

Cowards die many times before their deaths;
The valiant never taste of death but once.
Of all the wonders that I yet have heard,
It seems to me most strange that men should fear;
Seeing that death, a necessary end,
Will come when it will come.

Perhaps the final statement on dying well occurs in a short story about the Crucifixion when Hemingway has a Roman soldier say of Jesus, "He looked pretty good to me in there today."

Hemingway, finally, demands of the individual a certain version of courage and grace—not at all bad qualities to ask for. After "nada," the ritual of meaninglessness, what is left? Hemingway says sensitive sensuality (the solar joy), honor, competence, courage—and that's quite a lot. Taken together, these apparently simple capacities form a rudimentary version of mental well-being. The hero functions, and functions effectively. Indeed, Hemingway's idea of competence prefigures recent thinking by psychologists and sociologists that identifies the urge toward mastering one's environment and finding pleasurable involvement in activity for its own sake as a central feature of human healthiness.

The Author as Hero

In a loving and gently perceptive memoir about the writers of Hemingway's generation, *A Second Flowering*, Malcolm Cowley observes that the artists who were young in the 1920s shared a bold faith in their vocation.

The good writers regarded themselves as an elite, a word that later came to be a sneer. They were an elite not by birth or money or education, not even by acclaim—though they would have it later—but rather by such inner qualities as energy, independence, vision, rigor, an original way of combining words (a style, a "voice"), and utter commitment to a dream. Those qualities they grouped together as their "talent," about which they spoke as if it were something precariously in their possession, a blooded animal, perhaps, to be fed, trained, guarded carefully, and worked to the limit of its power, but not beyond. . . . For one thing, they tried to be accurate observers of their age; for another, they regarded their talent as something apart from their ordinary selves. Hence, their efforts to preserve the talent were selfless, after a fashion, or at least ran counter in many cases to their material interests. A question they asked themselves was "How can I best live in order to produce the books that are in me?"[9]

In these themes of high seriousness about the writer's role Hemingway is exemplary. If he played to the hilt a public role as "great American novelist" and was much concerned to present himself to his readers as dashing and courageous, he never forgot that his chief task lay in the more private enactment of creative skill. Few writers have been so articulate about the lonely and awe-provoking aspects of their vocation; he speaks frequently of the stress, the self-doubts, the stamina required to set experience down as truly and as transparently as possible. A thorough professional, Hemingway studied the techniques of great writers, consciously compared himself to them, and adhered faithfully to his very strict self-erected standards of honesty and accuracy. Until almost the very end of his life, he showed a remarkable durability, holding himself to the job and throwing himself fully into story after story. Above all, he had the stubborn courage to return daily to face the typewriter—to face himself—and wrench from the flux of existence a pattern of integrity. In this he represents the vitality, the love of words, and the capacity for self-interrogation that distinguish the poet alive.

Hemingway was an exceedingly self-conscious writer who knew precisely what he was doing. One might say that, among his peers, Fitzgerald, Faulkner, and Wolfe were often possessed by their material; but Hemingway possessed his. He knew his demon and controlled it. This is demonstrated in his concern for literary strategies and tactics and in his recurrent use of sporting and military metaphors to describe what it was like to write. He always sounds as if sitting down to the typewriter were like going into battle. He compares himself to noted predecessors in terms of who can get in the boxing ring together and who will get knocked out. And these metaphors contain their truths. Writing *is* a kind of combat; it is a struggle to get things down exactly on paper in the one best fashion out of all conceivable fashions. The combat is the more arduous in that the author's adversary is intangible, a composite ghost of self-knowledge and clear perception and carven language. Any good writer's path takes him through a minefield of temptations: to be sloppy, to use the easy word, to be less than honest, to let the inexact expression serve. A much gentler man than Hemingway, the English poet Stephen Spender, also describes the job in terms of struggle; Spender says that in writing a poem one is "wrestling with a god." As it might be observed, too, writing is essentially an aritificial act, and Hemingway's view of the novelist as a kind of aesthetic athlete may have been an attempt both to render this act more natural and to bolster his own creative courage.

Not content to portray himself as engaged literary man, Hemingway went beyond to cultivate a careful public image in which he acted and spoke in the manner of his own heroes. In this he was, of course, not alone. Fitzgerald did it too, as did many of the Romantics much earlier. But Fitzgerald's heroes are youthful and introspective, and he was unable to sustain the image of the self as hero in the face of his personal torments and his ageing. In the same era, several writers chose to be resolutely private men—notably Faulkner and T. S. Eliot. Hemingway, however, felt constrained to devise a role as a versatile man of the world who happened, not at all incidentally, to be a great writer. Another successful inventor of a mask for dealing with the world of men was George Bernard Shaw; his youthful design is akin to Hemingway's as this account shows: "Whether it be that I was born mad or a little too sane, my kingdom was not of this world: I was at home only in the realm of my imagination, and at my ease only with the mighty dead. Therefore I had to become an actor, and create for myself a fantastic personality fit and apt for dealing with men, and adaptable to the various parts I had to play as author, journalist, orator, politician, committee man, man of the world, and so forth."[10] Shaw goes on to note that in some ways he succeeded only too well, that for his public the mask became the man and was later in his career an artifice that needed living up to. So Hemingway devised an image of the male adventurer, the man among men, whose competence was multifaceted. He became the adept sportsman—hunting, fishing, boxing, and swimming, always with a measured skill. He became the soldier—war correspondent, never content to be anywhere but where the action was. He became lover and protector of a series of women. He reveled in the companionship of the bottle and scorned less heroic drinkers. And at length, weathered and fond of the gnomic utterance, he became "Papa," the bearded sage.

It has been rather convincingly asserted that Hemingway's person was a tangle of psychiatric problems. Surely there is a driven quality to his exhibitions of compulsive masculinity, his fictions of invulnerability, and his contempt for the weak. The Yaloms contend that at last it was the impossibility of living up to this exaggerated self-picture that led to dissolution and suicide: "At the end, the union of the psychological central identity and the grandiose peripheral system fragmented: Hemingway's inner core, naked and vulnerable, pervaded his experiential world. Consumed with feelings of guilt and worthlessness he sunk deep into despair."[11] But the truth of psychiatric disability has to be set beside the truth of artistic integrity and commitment. Malcolm Cowley's last word on Hemingway is perhaps the best word.

Handicapped as the old lion was by injuries and admirers, tormented by demons from the subconscious, he continued almost to the end a double life, playing the great man in public—even at the Mayo Clinic, where he played the part superbly for the doctors—then standing alone at his writing table, humble and persistent, while he tried to summon back his early powers. . . . As we retrace the story, Hemingway's private or writing self becomes distinct from his shadow side, and it seems to us more appealing than his admired and debated persona. There is one respect and only one in which he resembled Hart Crane, who was born on the same day and whom he outlasted by nearly thirty years. Both of them felt that if they couldn't write, they didn't want to live.[12]

Hemingway and the Age

It is doubtful Hemingway would have well understood or sympathized with many of the chief American preoccupations of the last decade. The controversies about South Vietnam, the drug culture, Watergate, or women's liberation seem quite remote from his world. He was very much a man of his times, and those times were characterized by more confidence, more exuberance, and clearer-cut models of social roles and values than have been vouchsafed to us. Hemingway's generation of writers thought of themselves as a vanguard, inheritors of a fresh new world where anything was possible; freed alike from stale literary conventions and the provincialism of manners and morals in turn-of-the-century United States, they felt themselves on the edge of discovery. Yearning for greatness and entirely convinced that the writer's role was of vital significance in human affairs, Hemingway displayed an appetite for living and a certitude about right and wrong in conduct that are today both appealing and somewhat foreign.

In three sectors, especially, it is instructive to see where Hemingway stands and what the distance between that stance and our own implies about American social changes. The novelist is most explicit about the roles of men and women, the values attached to vocational striving, and the place of warfare in the lives of men and nations. For him, partly as a consequence of certain events in his early life but more fully as a result of his accepting the norms of his time, male and female roles were well-defined and complementary. The man appears as dominant and protective, the woman as submissive, dependent, loving. Brett Ashley, Hemingway's nearest approach to a fully drawn and free woman, is really free only in her irresponsibility; and Brett is clearly intended to be seen as extraordinary, a sport thrown off by a decaying aristocracy. His other heroines tend to be one-dimensional, actually appendages to the men around whom the action pivots. The heroes are thoroughly involved in a world of other men and other activities, so much so that loving a woman becomes merely an interlude, however significant, and is finally of transitory importance. Here, then, we find one vital difference in role definitions, and one against which today's young reader properly rebels. Perhaps the prototypical expression of Hemingway's version of relations between the sexes is the affair between Robert Jordan and the Spanish girl Maria in *For Whom the Bell Tolls*. Here Jordan is plainly the master; the girl passes briefly in and out of his life, and their pairing is subject both to his momentary desires and to his larger political and military vocations.

The center of a man's social universe in Hemingway's stories, as in his own life, is not to be found in love or parenthood, friendship, or citizenship. Rather, it lies in the doing of something well, the exercise of a styled competence toward an external goal, whether the object be nature, language, or sport. Beside a man's vocation, all else is rendered trivial. The overriding charge to the individual is to be excellent in an activity and to take it with high seriousness. Such commitment, although not as alien to us as his model of male-female relationships, is nevertheless muted in the culture of the late twentieth century. A single-minded focus on masculine performance, in an atmosphere of striving and failing, winning and losing, no longer seems quite so important. Indeed, the reader, especially the younger reader, questions the worth of sheer competitiveness as the preferred mode of confronting the world. He asks about the negative side effects of such exclusive concentration on a narrow performance, the way in which vocational striving may distract attention and energy from matters that may be of equal or greater significance in the total round of experience.

Not unrelated to the stress on activity and courageous competence for its own sake is Hemingway's mixed but zestful attitude toward war. He is under no illusion that warfare solves human problems; Frederic Henry bolts from the confusion and injustice of the Italian campaign, and Robert Jordan in the Spanish Civil War discovers betrayal and witless brutality as well as heroism. Yet wars are seen as worth the fighting, however senselessly they eventuate in any grand design or long run. And they are worth the fighting precisely because they afford a man a stage, an ultimate arena for testing his endurance and grace. Once more we may observe that the thirst for military action, the urge to be at the scene of violent encounters, appears to be a sharply declining value in modern society. Yet Hemingway, in his novels and in his own forays to three battlefronts as ambulance driver and newspaper correspondent, is an authentic spokesman for an earlier and more innocent era of our national life.

But if Hemingway is firmly bonded to the first half of this century and if many of his assumptions are now unfashionable, we must still recognize that the universal qualities of his themes and perceptions outweigh the time bound. Regardless of changes in a society's values or in its conceptions of social roles, the key issues of being human and living a life persist. Whatever the specific lineaments of the social universe, one can scarcely envision a model of the good life that is not instinct with Hemingway's virtues. The individual cannot move through this world, cannot count himself fully alive, without the sense of solar joy, without the exercise of competence, without some deep apprehension of fidelity to himself and others. William James said that the true gentleman was the person who, in sure knowledge of life's brevity, yet conducted himself as if he were going to live forever. This the writer must do, especially in the conduct of his writing. So the best part of Hemingway lives on in the clear language, if not forever, at least for a very long time.

4

Arthur Miller

The Salesman and Society

In The Smoking Car

The eyelids meet. He'll catch a little nap.
The grizzled, crew-cut head drops to his chest.
It shakes above the briefcase on his lap.
Close voices breathe, "Poor sweet, he did his best."

"Poor sweet, poor sweet," the bird-hushed glades repeat,
Through which in quiet pomp his litter goes,
Carried by native girls with naked feet.
A sighing stream concurs in his repose.

Could he but think, he might recall to mind
The righteous mutiny or sudden gale
That beached him here; the dear ones left behind . . .
So near the ending, he forgets the tale.

Were he to lift his eyelids now, he might
Behold his maiden porters, brown and bare.
But even here he has no appetite.
It is enough to know that they are there.

Enough that now a honeyed music swells,
The gentle, mossed declivities begin,
And the whole air is full of flower-smells.
Failure, the longed-for valley, takes him in.

Richard Wilbur

When failure takes Willy Loman in, we are obliged to follow him into the "longed-for valley," for we are all implicated in Willy's dream of success and his nightmare of defeat. Shaw, commenting upon the domestic drama of Ibsen, points out that we cannot be detached or merely amused; referring to the play within a play in *Hamlet*, Shaw calls the audience "guilty creatures sitting at a play." Why do we feel guilty? Why is *Death of a Salesman* so painfully close to home that we flinch and weep for our parents, and perhaps for ourselves? I suggest that the immense power of Arthur Miller's American tragedy is rooted in two primary sources: the psychological depth in which he explores family relationships, and his sociological grasp of certain fundamental elements of life, particularly occupational life, in the United States.

The Psychodynamic Elements

Daniel Schneider, in his remarkably perceptive study *The Psychoanalyst and the Artist*, finds the heart of the play in the relationship between the salesman, Willy, and his two sons. He starts with the symbol of the heavy sample cases that weigh on Willy as the play begins: "There is at the outset a cogent symbolization of the substance of the play: the salesman comes home carrying wearily the two battered, black sample cases that are his cross. They are like the two sons he has carried through life; they are a burden we want him to set down with honor, but we sense almost at once that they are to be his coffin."[1]

Schneider sees the presentation of historical events in the play, for example the conversations with Willy's older brother Ben or Biff's afternoon of football glory, as hallucinations in the present rather than as flashbacks to the past. These hallucinations constitute the return of the repressed, in psychoanalytic terms the invasion of the ego by primitive impulse. Here is the inrush of the unconscious self, unknowingly compromised and buried; it is the return Jung so terrifyingly characterized as "with knife in hand." Weakened by fatigue and oppressed by his lengthening catalogue of failures, Willy becomes increasingly vulnerable and disorganized. What we witness is a human being coming apart before our eyes. In Willy's own words, "The woods are burning!"

Is Willy's disintegration the stuff of classic tragedy? Clearly, Willy is not in actuality noble or larger than life. But he is a hero in his dreams, and this play is after all concerned with a variety of feckless dreams. One might even contend that twentieth-century American society differs from the society of Aristotle's *Poetics* precisely in that here and now all men are enjoined to seek the enoblement of economic achievement. In any event, Willy is, in Meredith's fine phrase, "betrayed by what is false within." And he is betrayed, of course, not only by his own intrinsic flaws but by the manifold falsenesses he has long encouraged in his sons. There is an inevitability about his collapse that is beautifully caught by Schneider's comparison of the sample cases to coffins.

Schneider isolates the sons' disillusionment with their father as the dominant conflict in the play. Willy is a god who decays before the boys' eyes, a decay strikingly shown in Biff's collapse after he finds his father in a Boston hotel room with a mistress. The father has been sexless in being godlike, and this image is now destroyed. Schneider sees this as a variation of the Oedipal theme: the father has played god (for instance, in "fixing" things for the growing boys when they run into trouble, the trouble having arisen in part from the sons' efforts to follow Willy's warped dicta for "success") and then fails to measure up to godhood. One might add the reciprocal disillusionment of Willy with his sons, a revelation so hard to bear that in panic he adopts every strategy for concealing it from himself. Like all families, the Lomans share certain almost essential fictions about one another; but since their fictions are exaggerated and grotesque, the truth is correspondingly painful in intensity. The mute conspiracy that supports the fictions and the devastation brought by the unmasking are astonishingly similar to the themes of the family drama in O'Neill's *Long Day's Journey Into Night*.

Willy's steady fall in the second act, when he is told he is no good as a salesman and simultaneously is driven to face his sons' unworthiness, culminates in symbolic murder. Instead of having an anticipated celebration dinner at which Willy's authority and old paternal role might be reaffirmed, the father and sons break up: Willy is symbolically castrated and rushes to the bathroom while the sons assert their own sexuality by picking up two girls.

The mother accuses the sons of killing their father by their whoring. Schneider discovers in this sequence the ancient archetypal drama celebrated in the Oedipus myth and in Freud's notion of the primal horde. "This is as close to the original battle fought eons ago by man and his sons as has ever been put upon the stage. It is this very thinly and yet very adroitly disguised Oedipal murder which gives the play its peculiar symbolic prehistoric power. It is not only modern man exploited; it is also Neanderthal man raging against the restraint of civilization's dawn."[2]

Finally, Schneider thinks the tragedy is concerned with a hidden motivation—the guilt of a younger son for hating his older brother. Willy envies the rich and mysterious Ben; Hap envies Biff. Willy's failure is in the defeat of his effort to overtake Ben by becoming a successful salesman. "In a sense," the psychoanalyst says, "every first son 'strikes it rich' in a younger son's eyes."[3]

This psychodynamic analysis, then, treats the play as primarily a family drama, attentive to unconscious motivations and preeminently psychological in import. Schneider sees the social conflicts as secondary and external to the clash of character and the working out of timeless universal forces. He says relatively little about the American society and the American values that constitute the environment of the family plot. But I shall argue that the society in which the Lomans move is more than a fortuitous historical frame, that its nature is integral to the action of the play. Willy's role as salesman is equal in significance to, and in the end inseparable from, his role as father and husband. For here the public and the private, the domestic and the occupational worlds, merge, and are alike confounded by Willy's posturing dreams.

The Necessity to Strive

Willy with his sample cases is not only the father, with his burdensome sons, parental responsibilities, and vast vulnerabilities. He is also, and as importantly, a salesman sui generis. Those cases straining his arms and seeming to drain him of vitality are not merely symbols; they contain real goods for sale, and Willy in trying to peddle them is a pathetic archetype of the American dream of success. Despite the fact that most Americans are not salesmen by a strict occupational definition, that, unlike Willy, we work in large organizations and are hourly or salaried employees, we have in all of us something of the salesman and dream his dream of a success obtained through individual desire and energy. What Erich Fromm termed the "marketing orientation" is woven into the fabric of our national life; in this disposition of personality, the individual's credo is "I am as you desire me." So Willy attempts to be the person he thinks others desire: for his customers, the jovial yet dignified drummer; for his sons, the firm yet indulgent and all-protective father; for his wife, the ever-dependable breadwinner. He tells Biff and Happy about his friends: "And they know me, boys, they know me up and down New England. The finest people. And when I bring you fellas up, there'll be open sesame for all of us, 'cause one thing, boys: I have friends. I can park my car in any street in New England, and the cops protect it like their own."[4] In this society we all feel, more or less keenly, that we must sell ourselves, must be responsive to the demands of others, must make a good impression in order to be (as Willy puts it) not just "liked, but *well*-liked."

When we see *Death of a Salesman* we are truly "guilty creatures at a play." Willy's failure is our failure, for we are also involved in the cult of success, and we, too, measure men by occupational attainment rather than by some sympathetic calculus of the whole human being. We are all partners in the American Dream and parties to the conspiracy of silence surrounding the fact that failures must by definition outnumber successes, given our cultural ground rules and our singular interpretations of the words "success" and "failure." Surely part of the undeniable power Miller's play exerts is rooted in the author's audacity in breaking this conspiracy of silence, in revealing to us a failure almost too painful for audiences to bear. How many times has one heard contemporaries exclaim that Willy reminds them of their own fathers, and that they find a deep loving sorrow in the reminiscence. One of the master themes in twentieth-century American literature is the articulation of the individual's quest for a vocational identity and a satisfying public image of self with the private world of family relationships. O'Neill, Fitzgerald, Hemingway—all grapple with the devilish ambiguities and profound disappointments that seem intrinsic to the striving for success and its attendant lack of domestic tranquillity.

Success and Failure

We need to look more closely into the nature of success and into its social context in the United States. In this effort we can begin with a model first advanced by Robert K. Merton in his germinal essay "Social Structure and Anomie."[5] Merton distinguishes two major features of the social structure—cultural goals and institutional norms. Cultural goals consist of the ends toward which we strive, in Willy Loman's case the image of the master salesman, esteemed by all and almost effortlessly able to move his goods and earn a comfortable living. Thus Willy remembers his early ambition to seek his fortune in Alaska and what redirected him toward the life of a salesman.

And I was almost decided to go, when I met a salesman in the Parker House. His name was Dave Singleman. And he was eighty-four years old, and he'd drummed merchandise in thirty-one states. And old Dave, he'd go up to his room, y'understand, put on his green velvet slippers— I'll never forget—and pick up his phone and call the buyers, and without ever leaving his room, at the age of eighty-four, he made his living. And when I saw that, I realized that selling was the greatest career a man could want. 'Cause what could be more satisfying than to be able to go, at the age of eighty-four, into twenty or thirty different cities, and pick up a phone, and be remembered and loved and helped by so many different people? Do you know? when he died—and by the way he died the death of a salesman, in his green velvet slippers in the smoker of the New York, New Haven and Hartford, going into Boston— when he died, hundreds of salesmen and buyers were at his funeral. Things were sad on a lot of trains for months after that.[6]

Willy's goal, then, reiterated in many guises throughout the course of the play, is to achieve as a salesman; but perhaps more important, it is to be "remembered and loved and helped by so many different people."

Merton asserts, "Aberrant behavior may be regarded sociologically as a symptom of dissociation between culturally prescribed aspirations and sociologically structured avenues for realizing those aspirations."[7] Willy finds that available institutional norms, or "structured avenues," are not open to him. Unable to discover the means to realize himself as a latter-day Dave Singleman, he does indeed become aberrant, but in a fashion we find all too poignantly understandable. Willy exemplifies the dissociation between goals and means that Merton identifies: "Contemporary American culture appears to approximate the polar type in which great emphasis upon certain success goals occurs without equivalent emphasis upon institutional means."[8]

Merton's argument is essentially that American emphasis on success—particularly as gauged by the accumulation of wealth—outruns the availability of means for achieving success, at least among large sectors of the population. Individuals in the lower-middle and lower social strata are especially exposed to this discrepancy, and the lower-middle class is of course precisely Willy Loman's milieu. All audiences of *Death of a Salesman* are aware of Willy's unrealistic dreams, his half-knowing deception of himself and others. He harbors inflated hopes for his own success. When the hopes must be relinquished, when he is reduced to begging for "a little salary," they still persist in displaced form as dreams for his sons' achievements. Here he is entirely consistent with the familiar parental syndrome of projecting success hopes upon one's children; to pass the baton to the next runner in this fashion is also consonant with the stress on the unceasing struggle for achievement and on the assumption of individual responsibility for one's vocational destiny. Willy knows in very general terms where he wants to go—to be rich like his elder brother, Ben, or to be revered like Dave Singleman. But he hasn't the faintest idea of how to get there. Quite prepared to sell himself as well as his goods to pursue the chimera of being universally well liked, Willy lacks the interpersonal competence on which he pins his faith just as he lacks the technical competence to make big sales. He cannot adopt a meaningful strategy for achievement; stale slogans—"The world is an oyster, but you don't crack it open on a mattress!"—are the failing substitute for intelligent planning or commercial skill. As one of my affluent Ivy League undergraduates once disdainfully expressed it, "Willy just doesn't pack the gear." Yet the point is perhaps not to condemn the foolishness of his great expectations.

It is, rather, to analyze the origins of the dream, the imperative for clinging to it in the face of overwhelmingly negative evidence, and the tenacity with which Willy holds his system of beliefs. Who taught this man to hope so gloriously, to dream so boldly?

Our culture has consistently exhorted the individual to strive for transcendent success. Today's inciting langauge is probably less vulgar (and also less honest) than the strident nineteenth-century pronouncements of an Andrew Carnegie—"Say each to yourself: 'My place is at the top.' Be king in your dreams"—or a Russell H. Conwell—"I say that you ought to get rich, and it is your duty to get rich"; "The idea is that in this country of ours every man has the opportunity to make more of himself than he does in his own environment, with his own skill, with his own energy, and with his own friends." But one may doubt that the substance of the message has changed much. The transition from Andrew Carnegie to Dale Carnegie, epitomized by David Riesman as "from the invisible hand to the glad hand," entails less emphasis on capital formation and more on the charms of leadership style, but the aim is still to be a winner in a very competitive game, whose rules are as vague as its scoreboard is explicit. In Merton's axiom of striving, one should regard the situation as fluid, never foreclosing one's chances, and should identify oneself with those at the top whom one will sooner or later join. And we are enjoined, further, to think that energetic ambition is in some sense a moral obligation, a responsibility devolving solely on the individual, to be honored even in the situation of patent failure.

Willy Loman is an exemplar of just these values. In fact, each of the figures in *Death of a Salesman* may be viewed as enmeshed in this set of circumstances, and each takes some path of action in the effort to deal with them. Merton sets forth a number of alternate strategies an individual might adopt in trying to cope with the American success ethic. He arranges them in a seemingly simple but remarkably stimulating model:

Comformity—accepting both conventional cultural goals and approved institutional means of reaching them
Innovation—accepting the goals but rejecting the fully legitimate means

Ritualism—rejecting or withdrawing from the goals, but dutifully
    adhering to the means
Retreatism—shunning both the goals and the means; essentially,
    not playing the game
Rebellion—substituting new values in the realms of both goals
    and means

Obviously, very few people could be expected to cling uniformly
to a single one of these strategies throughout life; almost all
actual behavior is composed of mixed strategies, and people
shift their emphases in tune with life's exigencies. Nevertheless,
it is fair to say that each of Miller's characters seizes one of
these patterns as his dominant mode for coming to grips with
the imperatives of success. A brief sketch of their choices may
supplement Schneider's psychological analysis of the drama—
the love and hate among brothers, fathers, and sons—with a
sociological context.

Willy Loman's path is primarily that of conformity. Indeed,
one of the saddest aspects of his story lies in his stubborn, futile
effort to do what is expected of him; then, having played by the
rules as he conceives them and having held a bright image of
achievement in mind, he is unfairly deprived of his just reward.
Thus Willy laments, in dialogue with his wife:

WILLY: Figure it out. Work a lifetime to pay off a house. You
    finally own it, and there's nobody to live in it.
LINDA: Well, dear, life is a casting off. It's always that way.
WILLY: No, no, some people—some people accomplish some-
    thing.[9]

Especially in his earlier years, Willy embraces the dominant
values of his culture and struggles to reach them through legitimate techniques. He has never really *been* very successful, but he
has admired those who made it and he has held out hope. His
sense of the imperative is so overpowering that he is forced to lie
to himself and his sons, to buck himself up with a threnody of
exhortation and might have been. He doggedly believes in his
society as the land of opportunity. But Willy does not realize that
"personality" and friendship are not enough. In the contemporary United States occupational conduct is more clearly gov-

erned by "universalism" (not who you are, but what you can do) and "functional specificity" (not the valuing of the total man, but of his specific skills and contributions to some enterprise). So Willy's best friend Charley tries to enlighten him:

WILLY: Charley, I'm strapped. I'm strapped. I don't know what to do. I was just fired.

CHARLEY: Howard fired you?

WILLY: That snotnose. Imagine that? I named him. I named him Howard.

CHARLEY: Willy, when're you gonna realize that them things don't mean anything? You named him Howard, but you can't sell that. The only thing you got in this world is what you can sell. And the funny thing is that you're a salesman, and you don't know that.

WILLY: I've always tried to think otherwise, I guess. I always felt that if a man was impressive, and well liked, that nothing—

CHARLEY: Why must everybody like you? Who liked J. P. Morgan? Was he impressive? In a Turkish bath he'd look like a butcher. But with his pockets on he was very well liked.[10]

Willy, however, cannot bring himself to understand. He talks of his n'er-do-well older son, Biff: "Biff Loman is lost. In the greatest country in the world a young man with such personal attractiveness, gets lost."[11]

As life closes in on him in the form of time payments, disappointing children, failing energies, and the bald truth that the Dave Singleman legend is not to be his, Willy slips more nearly into *ritualism*. He still plays the game and abides by the rules but doesn't truly hope for economic success; he emphasizes his manual talents more strongly and his wish to raise chickens at a little place in the country. Finally he follows an unusual form of *innovation*: desperately wanting the success goals for his sons, he uses illegitimate means to provide them with money—that is, the proceeds of his life insurance policy, the only tangible thing he has to give them. From another perspective, Willy's suicide could be seen as the ultimate in *retreatism*, the final turning away from a life and a society that have perhaps failed him as much as he has failed them. Suicide, given Willy's hopes for his boys and his dutifulness toward his wife, may be for him the closest approximation of the more common kinds of retreatism such as Skid Row.

Willy's friend and neighbor, Charley, exemplifies *conformity*, accepting both the goal of success and the approved routes to its attainment. He and his son, Bernard, form a counterpoint to Willy and his boys; Charley and Bernard are realists, appraising their circumstance with clear eye and hard head. Their facility in "making it" is presented to us in recurrent contrast to the windy, aimless thrashing about of the Lomans, impaled between dreams and incompetence. We are offered few details of Charley's successful coping. He appears as a shrewd if largely unheeded counselor to Willy, and as a businessman comfortable enough to subsidize Willy's declining months. Bernard's career, traced in somewhat more detail, is the classic American success story of our era. Thematically, it is sharply opposed to the drifting non-careers of Biff and Happy Loman. At least two facets of Bernard's history are especially significant in the light of contemporary social structure. The first is the value he places on education, which is, as we know, more and more often *the* path to occupational achievement. Bernard learns his lessons well; he is groomed by the school system and his parents to value both academic attainment per se and the complex of motivations surrounding it. A "good boy" conforming to all expectations, he reaps a good boy's rewards. The second striking element in Bernard is the symbolic import of his career, the meaning of appearing as a lawyer before the Supreme Court. Here Miller has chosen both a high-prestige profession—in some ways today the case type of conforming careerism—and an institution, the Supreme Court, that stands at the very peak of American occupational esteem. Finally, the scene between Bernard and Willy in Charley's office and the ensuing conversation Willy has with Charley underline again the distinctions between a fulfilling and an unfulfilling conformity. We have once more the contrast of charm versus competence, seeming versus doing.

WILLY: The Supreme Court! And he didn't even mention it!
CHARLEY: He don't have to—he's gonna do it.[12]

Willy's brother, Ben, represents *innovation* in Merton's analysis. He has fully adopted the goal of material success but has apparently taken unusual and not entirely approved means to realize the goal. He has gone outside the framework of his society as an adventurer in the Alaska of that day, presumably the twenties and thirties. His business ethics are questionable, as indicated in the scene in which he trips Biff with his cane and comments, "Never fight fair with a stranger, boy. You'll never get out of the jungle that way."[13] Like many innovators—the Robber Barons of the late nineteenth century, the gangsters of the twentieth—Ben has a glamorous aura. People like Ben have often been admired in American life, especially by the conforming or ritualistic Willys, who see in the Bens a confirmation of the cultural promise. Thus Willy describes Ben's success: "What's the mystery? The man knew what he wanted and went out and got it! Walked into a jungle, and comes out, the age of twenty-one, and he's rich!"[14]

It is true, as Schneider observes, that the heart of *Death of a Salesman* is the complex relationships between Willy and his sons and between the two sets of brothers (Willy and Ben, Biff and Happy). The dynamics of this interplay, punctuated by affection, jealousy, high expectations and cruel recriminations, are the threads that lead us through Willy's disaster. But the primary sociological point is these relationships all find their focus, their emotional field of force, in the occupational world and the success ethic. We have seen how Willy and Ben take different paths and how Ben represents for Willy a brutal, flashy alternative to the success image of Dave Singleman. How do Biff and Happy respond to the challenges inherent in Merton's model of ends and means?

The Loman brothers grow up nourished by their father's misguided but potent success dream. Throughout their lives Willy devotes himself to coaching them, almost like an older teammate, in the techniques for winning the striving game. He stresses, of course, those tactics he believes to be the keys to achievement: popularity, congeniality, physical prowess, attractiveness—in a phrase, the cult of personality. Willy never tells the boys they need skill or industriousness; indeed, he sedulously encourages them, especially Biff, in cutting corners and relying on personal magnetism to carry the day. One might say he determinedly sells them the bill of goods he has once been sold, infecting the next generation with the vocational pathology whose symptoms bring him down.

Biff, the older son, appears to fit the pattern of *retreatism*. We feel occasionally that if Biff had more energy and stability of purpose he might pursue *rebellion*; yet his rebellion only flickers in the desert of his nomadic drifting, as in his dream of an outdoor life far from the rat race. Although Biff pays sporadic lip service to the cultural goals, partly in a futile effort to buck up the sagging Willy, he really has withdrawn his allegiance from both common goals and common means. His wandering in the West is an escape from the competitive occupational world, just as it is an escape from the father whose infidelity makes him feel sexually betrayed. He vaguely yearns for something different but does not have the qualities to articulate and search out that "something." Biff's attitudes and behavior add up to a bitter caricature of a man, trapped by the success ethic, floundering as his father flounders: "I tell ya, Hap, I don't know what the future is. I don't know—what I'm supposed to want. . . . And always to have to get ahead of the next fella. And still—that's how you build a future. . . . I've always made a point of not wasting my life, and everytime I come back here I know that all I've done is to waste my life."[15]

Happy seems harder to place in Merton's terms but is generally *conforming*. Although his sharp business practices may incline toward *innovation* on the style of his Uncle Ben, his is a kind of empty conformity. Happy gets, in modest measure, what he thinks he wants, but his life is somehow flavorless, without bite or savor. He is the one character many critics of the play have found puzzling and inconsistent with the master themes of the drama. Schneider goes so far as to suggest that the play might be seen as a dream of Happy, that he stands outside the main flow of action.

Linda, wife and mother, is obviously the linchpin that holds the Loman family together, as nearly as they may be said to cohere. Of course, in her role she does not confront the occupational strife as a direct participant; nevertheless, the strains of all three male Lomans lap over into her life. Hers is the voice of sweet reason, of the wise, resigned observer. But with all her understanding of what makes Willy run, she is powerless to stop the onrush of failure and doom. Linda's chosen path is *ritualism*. She keeps on keeping on but asks wearily, "Why must everybody conquer the world?"[16]

Final Comparisons

One might argue, with justice, that *Death of a Salesman*'s only peer as *the* American play of the twentieth century is Eugene O'Neill's *Long Day's Journey Into Night*. As I noted earlier, there are many thematic similarities in the two. They are, of course, "about" the same thing—life-long quest of a certain image of self and other, set in the twin frameworks of family role relationships and occupational success striving. Both demonstrate how these spheres interpenetrate, particularly the way in which a culturally enjoined success ethic informs and corrodes family life. The Lomans and the Tyrones, though unlike in many ways, are both nuclear families and almost totally self-absorbed. The family members, with few ties to any rich life outside, feed upon one another; demanding too much of one another and of themselves, they are embittered by the inevitable gulf between ideal image and functioning reality. Both families subsist on fictions, shared delusions that seem necessary to the preservation of any family life at all. Perhaps all families require the maintenance of certain myths about themselves; but the Tyrones and the Lomans are extraordinary in the pervasiveness and grandeur of their domestic myths. In each play, crises arise and create a breaking through of the delusive fabric. Thus Biff, at last determined to expose Willy's comforting lies for what they are, says, "We never told the truth for ten minutes in this house!"[17] The dramas are also akin in that the action pivots on a troubled target member—Willy Loman, Mary Tyrone—whose torments throw the tangle of domestic affection and accusation into sharp relief.

In the end, Willy's tragedy lies as much in the bringing down of his dreams as in the bringing down of the man. In some curious way, perhaps the dreams were the best part of the man. Willy chased the same green light Jay Gatsby chased. Willy and Gatsby share the same epitaph—"nobody came to the funeral." Willy's whole being has been based on the moving power of a friendship and a presence that do not exist. And so his last dream of all comes to nothing: "Ben, that funeral will be massive! They'll come from Maine, Massachusetts, Vermont, New Hampshire! All the old-timers with the strange license plates—that boy will be thunderstruck, Ben, because he never realized—I am known! Rhode Island, New York, New Jersey—I am known, Ben, and he'll see it with his eyes once and for all. He'll see what I am, Ben!"[18]

Thomas Mann once remarked to Arthur Miller that *Death of a Salesman* is uniquely American in its directness, its transparency; everyman is here revealed to us in the simple, tangible story of a salesman who cannot sell. The play is now more than a quarter of a century old, and Willy Loman's America has been in many ways transformed. Yet the values portrayed and betrayed are with us still, and the pain and terror are not diminished by a fraction. Linda and Charley, who see Willy unblinkered, affirm that he is a tragic hero. Their words are now familiar, engraved on the consciousness of those who care about the American theatre and care about the texture of our national life:

LINDA: I don't say he's a great man. Willy Loman never made a lot of money. His name was never in the paper. He's not the finest character that ever lived. But he's a human being, and a terrible thing is happening to him. So attention must be paid. He's not to be allowed to fall into his grave like an old dog. Attention, attention must be finally paid to such a person. . . . A small man can be just as exhausted as a great man. . . .

CHARLEY: Nobody dast blame this man. You don't understand: Willy was a salesman. And for a salesman there is no rock bottom to the life. He don't put a bolt to a nut, he don't tell you the law or give you medicine. He's a man way out there in the blue, riding on a smile and a shoeshine. And when they start not smiling back—that's an earthquake. And then you get yourself a couple of spots on your hat, and you're finished. Nobody dast blame this man. A salesman is got to dream, boy. It comes with the territory. . . .

LINDA: Help me, Willy, I can't cry. It seems to me that you're just on another trip. I keep expecting you. Willy, dear, I can't cry. Why did you do it? I search and search and I can't understand it, Willy. I made the last payment on the house today. Today, dear. And there'll be nobody home. We're free and clear. We're free. We're free . . . We're free . . . [19]

5

Eugene O'Neill
The Web of Family

Eugene O'Neill's *Long Day's Journey Into Night* is by common consent the most important play of America's most important playwright. The day of the drama is very long; its hours, endlessly cycling in hope and disillusion, affection and disdain, are wearying to the sturdiest onlooker. We flinch from its candor; we shudder and are depressed. For here is art as a wrench, thrusting, goading, probing, and imposing on us what is in many ways a thoroughly uncomfortable experience. Yet the cathartic element of classical tragedy is abundantly present: we are curiously fascinated, cleansed, and finally calmed as fog and nightfall submerge the four Tyrones. As O'Neill said in his dedication of the play to his wife, Carlotta, it is a "play of old sorrow, written in tears and blood." But the dedication goes on to affirm, in a mood of noble resignation, that Carlotta has given him "the faith in love that enabled me to face my dead at last and write this play—write it with deep pity and understanding and forgiveness for all the four haunted Tyrones."[1] Hegel said: "History is what takes place behind our backs." So in *Long Day's Journey* O'Neill reaches boldly into his personal history for that understanding and resolution of the family drama that was impossible while its events were contemporary. In searching for the meaning of his domestic history, the author transmutes it into universal terms and confronts us with the family as society, a microcosm of interpersonal civility and brutality.

Long Day's Journey poses one of the classical problems in the relationship between the artist and his created world. How much of the drama is unique, idiosyncratic, and sheerly a projection of the author's personal torments? How much is the result of creative vision and wisdom and represents not only the joys and sorrows of O'Neill but something in the shared condition of modern man? We know that this was one of the most personal of writers, fighting his private battles on the stage, and that *Long Day's Journey* is one of the most genuinely autobiographical of all plays.

Is this shattering account to be experienced only clinically, as a product of the sickness and bitterness with which its author was consumed? Is the perhaps too facile wordplay on his name ("One Ill") quoted by a critic in *The Listener* a fair comment? There seems little doubt that O'Neill was in several respects an ill man. He attempted suicide, disrupted his most intimate personal ties, suffered what is euphemistically described in the language of his day as a "nervous breakdown," deserted responsibilities, was recurrently frightened by the fear of vocational failure. When young, he endured harsh physical illness (Tuberculosis), and later he experienced a neurological disability that made his last decade miserable and unproductive and finally killed him.

O'Neill surely exhibited, in unusually intense form, what the psychiatrist Karen Horney termed the "neurosis of our time"— a gnawing self-deprecation, sometimes approaching self-hatred, based on a wide gulf between the "is" and the "ought to be" or "might have been." As we shall see, this tension between the idealized self and the actual, "real," self also characterizes each of the Tyrones in *Long Day's Journey*. In his personal life, as in his literary career, O'Neill was persistently deviled by the felt failure to live up to some grander image. If ever a man felt a stranger and wanderer in a world he never made, felt the jarring disjunction between a glorious conception of his art and its inevitably compromised execution, felt the need to pose final moral questions, to which he never found answers—that man was O'Neill. Many critics have remarked on the curious groping quality in so much of his work, the attempt to deal with issues beyond his capacities of language or intellect. But at the same time, they note the severe honesty of his self-interrogation and the courage with which he faced the challenge of his art.

We know, of course, that the characters and events of *Long Day's Journey* are a roughly accurate parallel of the dramatist's own life history, his own family drama. O'Neill baldly states as much, and analysts of the play can cite dozens of examples. Clearly, Eugene O'Neill and the younger son in the play, Edmund Tyrone, share many experiences and philosophies. Both are marked by literary ambition, physical illness, periods of wandering about the world in a fuguelike state. Above all, both are trapped in a suffocating family milieu, one dominated by the temperament and the vocation of the father, the temperament and the addiction of the mother. The two potent background elements that steer the course of the action are identical in the O'Neills and Tyrones—the father's failed acting career, wrecked by a too easy and too lucrative success in a single long-running melodrama, and the peculiar conformations and deformations of Irish-American family culture.

I should maintain, nevertheless, that although this is a play about a distinctively sick family, written by one of its most badly wounded members, it is ultimately much more than a private nightmare. The author's craft and the resonance of his themes for all our lives make of *Long Day's Journey* a public nightmare. However absorbing its linkage to the facts of O'Neill's life, its linkage to central facets of the general human experience is more important. Irving Howe's wise comment on George Orwell's novel *1984* makes the point very persuasively.

Some people have suggested that *1984* is primarily a symptom of Orwell's psychological condition, the nightmare of a disturbed man who suffered from paranoid fantasies, was greatly troubled by dirt and feared that sexual contact would bring down punishment from those in authority. Apart from its intolerable glibness, such an "explanation" explains either too much or too little. Almost everyone has nightmares and a great many people have ambiguous feelings about sex, but few manage to write books with the power of *1984*. Nightmare the book may be, and no doubt it is grounded, as are all books, in the psychological troubles of its author. But it is also grounded in his psychological health, otherwise it could not penetrate so deeply the social reality of our time. The private nightmare, if it is there, is profoundly related to, and helps us understand, public events.[2]

As tragedy, the play conforms to many of the requirements laid down by Aristotle in the *Poetics*. Tragedy comes from within, from inner flaws of character; the action embraces the strict unities of time and space, with a single setting and a story concentrated in one seemingly endless twenty-four hours. It should be noted, though, that for the Tyrones the past is the present, so that this day's journey is actually a rehearsal of several decades, a catalogue of four twined life histories. The idea that tragedy flows from intrinsic defects of personality, rather than from the pressure of outer circumstance, is given contemporary expression by George Meredith in *Modern Love*:

In tragic life, God wot,
No villain need be! Passions spin the
    plot:
We are betrayed by what is false within.[3]

Mary Tyrone recognizes the unfolding of disfigured personal force in her reply to Tyrone's urging that she forget the past: "The past is the present, isn't it? It's the future, too. We all try to lie out of that but life won't let us."[4] O'Neill finds the locus of tragedy in inner weakness; his people never learn from their mistakes but are condemned to repeat them without end. Hence the quality of litany, of refrain, in all their speeches. These things are being said for the hundredth time, not the first, and they are repeated because the defects of personality are unchanging, fixed in amber and fortified by the drug alcohol or the drug morphine.

Yet the play is not without certain "fateful" occurrences, happenings that may owe part of their significance to blind accident. Tyrone's immense success in a single role, for instance, may be rooted in the availability of this appealing vehicle (*The Count of Monte Cristo*) and the American taste for melodrama at the turn of the century, as well as in his own hunger for money and security. Mary's addiction, too, is in one sense as much a result of medical bungling as of her desire to flee an unsatisfying marriage or to blot out her remorse over unrealized aspirations. If not quite everything is attributable to private pathology, then

Shakespeare's idea of the individual subjected to the whims of fortune is also present:

As flies to wanton boys are
   we to the gods;
They kill us for their sport.

In mounting a case for the play as valid tragedy, however, we face once more the key difficulty encountered with *Death of a Salesman*: the figures of the drama are neither noble nor larger than life. Classical theory asserts that tragedy can be truly moving only when the protagonist is a towering individual and his fall is from a great height of achievement or his splendidly formed personality deteriorates under the strain of its covert inadequacies. The problem of making ordinary—or even extraordinarily small and repellent—people into tragic heroes has often been singled out as a flaw in efforts to create modern tragedy. Yet, as with the collapse of Willy Loman, the descent of the four Tyrones does imbue us with the tragic spirit with its distinguishing moods of pity, catharsis, and a strange wild joy. I believe that, as in *Death of a Salesman*, a clue to the compelling quality of the "average man's" tragedy on stage may be found in the portrayal of him as dreaming of greatness, or at least of goodness. Each of the Tyrones has a dream, a vision of himself as better than he is. If this ideal of self were more pedestrian or were absent, the energizing tension between ideal and existing selves would disappear—and with it, I think, the heart of the play. In the end, as I shall discuss further below, the tragedy of *Long Day's Journey* represents a collective defeat, the decline and fall of a family system. Every member fails and falls separately, notably, of course, Mary, whose withdrawal from living is the motor of the action. But I view the four fates as finally one fate—the devolution of a network of interpersonal relations, the tearing apart of the web of family.

The Cultural Framework

This play was finished in 1941, but its setting is the New London of 1912. It is summer on the New England coast, the supposedly innocent and contented day of pre–World War I

America. Tyrone doesn't even drive his automobile, that unsettling new invention; the boys take a trolley car to go uptown.
All the horror, the corrosive failure of nerve, is imputed by
O'Neill to the modern consciousness *before* the age of world
wars and nuclear technology, the barbarisms of totalitarian societies, the true advent of mass society and massive social change.
The strains the family faces, then, lie too deep in character and
culture to be taken only as symptoms of the insecure generations
that followed 1918. Even if we grant that the author may have
projected into his family past something of the unsettled state of
1941 America, we had better try to discover consistent threads of
Western culture and family life that extend through several generations. These conflict-inspiring elements may be proposed to
frame and condition, if not indeed to determine, the individual
psychological dilemmas of the Tyrones.

We saw that the American success ethic, with its imperative
demand for some publicly validated achievement as symbol for
the validation of the self, was integral to each of the characters in
Death of a Salesman. And it is no less so for the Tyrones. James,
Mary, Jamie, Edmund—all are subject to very strong internal
urgencies for outstanding achievement. They habitually expect
great things from themselves and from one another; measuring
themselves against these failed hopes, they find slender satisfaction. Each is consumed with a bitter yearning for the might have
been. Disgust and self-contempt permeate the atmosphere of the
summerhouse that is all the Tyrones can call "home." Falling
short of the visions society has held out for him, the visions he
has adopted as his own appealing standards of the desirable,
each member of the family is his own harshest judge. And their
perceived failures are all the harder to accomodate because
these failures are made equivalent to moral worthlessness.

The elder Tyrone exemplifies the culturally phrased admonition to perform some valued role to the hilt, to the nether limits of
one's capacity. In his case, of course, it is quite literally a question of role attainment: his success in one stage part has been at
once so thorough and so limiting that he is unable to move
beyond it to a repertory more varied and more compelling. He
has, in fact, fulfilled the success ethic to a degree that would be
outwardly assessed as more than satisfactory. As a matinee idol,

Tyrone enjoys both the adulation and the piling up of material wealth that is its tangible fruit. Yet he has been told by no less a colleague than Booth that he had the talent to play the great roles, and he feels the waste of possibility, feels ridiculed and trapped. Tyrone's sustained need for achievement in his vocation as artist is thwarted by several things, notably by his lust for the competing goal of economic security: "What the hell was it I wanted to buy, I wonder, that was worth—Well, no matter. It's a late day for regrets."[5]

If Tyrone is the play's clearest case of the individual devoured by the success dream, the rest of the family parallel him in their chosen fashions. James and Mary, of course, teach their sons how to erect an exaggerated vision of self, and how to wallow in recriminations of self and others when the vision clouds. Mary's need for achievement is expressed in two rather different guises, her putative career chances as nun or musician and her vague but obsessive longing for some version of upper-middle-class domestic felicity. Her lament for the loss of these punctuates the action, serving at once as an alibi for her drug habit and an accusation of the other members. She plays, toward Tyrone, Jamie, and Edmund, a crafty game of what Eric Berne called "If It Weren't For You": if not for Tyrone's miserliness and life-style, Jamie's lazy appetites, Edmund's intrusive birth, her goals might have been reached. Although it is revealed that Mary's teachers were unconvinced she had an authentic religious vocation and that she may have had only mediocre promise as a pianist, these realities in no way undercut the strength of her dream or her felt guilt at its dissolution. Mary's yearning for domesticity, for a stable home of her own—one her men would not flee, and where friends could come to call—is also unrealized, and given the nature of family conflict, unrealizable.

Jamie's drive for achievement is perhaps the weakest among the Tyrones. He apparently has some talent as an actor, but he is always under his father's shadow. His self-destructive boozing and whoring, fueled by the posturing romanticism of the Mauve Decade, provide both an excuse for failure and an ample supply of guilt. Yet even Jamie is caught up in the success ethic and is contemptuous of himself for his indifferent performance. The elder son, Jamie, like the elder son, Biff, in *Death of a Salesman*, mirrors his father's worst qualities; even so, the fathers persist in the feckless hope that success can at length be retrieved for their errant firstborns. The second son, Edmund (Eugene), shows certain literary inclinations and a glimmering of poetic gifts. Despite his feel for apposite quotations from Baudelaire and Dowson and Wilde and his habitual introspection, Edmund remains fragile and unsure in his vision of self. Hence, like all the other members, he charges himself with relative failure. He professes to be inarticulate, the worst of handicaps for a poet, and disavows his talent, saying, "Stammering is the native eloquence of us fog people."[6]

Closely tied to the success ethic in American life is the money culture, the idea that the individual's worth may be reliably gauged in dollars and cents. For James Tyrone, the stress on economic competence that is so heavy in his adopted country is heightened by a background of poverty and by his Irish peasant roots. He is fundamentally convinced, in his brooding memory of a rural economy, that only the possession of land affords true dignity and ultimate security. Tyrone has learned the value of money too well, so well that his money has become a part of his personality and the thought of letting any of it go sickens and frightens him. His avarice and miserliness have their origins in an ancient insecurity, but they are fully significant only in the setting of the expansionary United States of the late nineteenth century. George Bernard Shaw announced that poverty is itself the worst of crimes, a condition poisonous to a fully human life. But Tyrone is not now poor; he has, rather, poisoned family life by his *fear* of poverty. As is so often true in a business society, money for the Tyrones becomes readily equated with love; when Tyrone withholds money, his family accuses him of withholding affection, caring, or concern. If Mary's losing battle with addiction is the manifest focus of the play, the others see Tyrone's winning battle with his bank accounts and land deeds as the covert cause of their misery, as the reason for Mary's illness, Edmund's consumption, and the failed dreams of all. What Tawney called "the sickness of an acquisitive society" is here plainly related to the sickness of a family group. And as with all the happenings of the Tyrones' past, everybody remembers everything. Each dollar not spent on medical care or housing, each dollar tossed away on acreage, is thrown up at Tyrone the breadwinner and life-loser.

To the cultural themes of the achievement need and the pathology of money must be added the peculiarly Irish elements that frame the Tyrone style of life. In a superbly revealing, if perhaps too dogmatic, essay "O'Neill's *Long Day's Journey Into Night* and New England Irish-Catholicism," John Henry Raleigh noted a cluster of these ethnic patterns that are woven through the play: "Excessively familial; noncommunal; sexually chaste; turbulent; drunken; alternately and simultaneously sentimental and ironical about love; pathologically obsessed with betrayal; religious-blasphemous; loquacious: these are some of the historical attributes of the Irish character."[7]

All of the attributes may be easily documented, but three of them merit special attention. These are the isolation and inwardness of the family unit, the ambiguities about social, and especially sexual, roles, and the confusion of values. For the Tyrones, the world outside the household scarcely exists; they are entirely absorbed in one another, lacking any other outlet for the heavy loads of affection and hostility they bear. We find no sense of community, neighborhood, or friendship. In this play no one ever comes to call. Mary traces the isolation to Tyrone's profession, an actor always on the road, and to his stinginess in never buying a decent house. However, we feel throughout that these people are simply too fascinated with each other, too tightly bound, to divert their attention outward. The nature of the closed family universe is underlined by the two fully adult sons' continuing to live at home and maintaining a primarily juvenile relationship with their parents. The family structure, then, is charged with meeting all the needs of all the members; each must be literally everything to each other. Thus Jamie says poignantly to Edmund, "You're the only pal I've ever had."[8]

The Tyrones seem to be unable to bring their various social roles into a coherent whole. The occupational world is split from the familial, the sexual from the affectionate. This dispersion and division is most strikingly shown in the behavior of the three men, who must recurrently flee from Mary in search of companionship, sex, or alcohol. The roles of male and female are isolated from one another because, first, occupation is defined as exclusively male, and second, the men embrace the stereotype so often found in a sexually repressive culture between the "good" woman and the "bad." Mary is "good," virginal and frigid. The men can share nothing of their passionate lives with her, and so they run off to the male comradery of club or bar, to the sexual release that can only be fulfilled with a "bad" woman like Jamie's fat tart. Indeed, Mary herself is never sure that she shouldn't have been a nun, never able to give herself undividedly as wife or mother. The Tyrones know everything about one another and are still strangers. Effective social role relationships are premised on minimal agreements among the parties to them about their respective rights and obligations; the Tyrones show no such mutuality.

The family is acutely subject to that confusion about values that distinguishes all modern societies in a rapidly changing world. Confronted with a wide range of choices and lacking any sure guide to priorities, the individual vacillates among competing images of the desirable. The confusion eventuates at the extreme, in the dread, dispirited state of valuelessness, a kind of moral paralysis in which no choice seems worthier than any other. Each Tyrone has held certain values strongly: the theatre, achievement, wealth and land, poetry, moral goodness, instinctual surcease through drugs or sex. Each has been thrown into conflict because of the clash of incompatible values, both within the self and vis-à-vis the rest of the family. And the conflicts are exacerbated by the process of acculturation, the effort to come to terms with the shift from rural Irish culture to urban American. Strains of acculturation are shown in many ways, perhaps especially in Tyrone's dedication to old peasant values while climbing the Yankee success ladder and in the family's allegiance to the family as a self-contained, self-sufficient group in an industrial society where this pattern is increasingly less workable. At the time of the play, no one appears to know any longer *what* to live for, although the father holds feebly to a failed Catholicism and the mother holds to a failed vision of genteel domesticity. Goals and the means of reaching them are ill coordinated; life becomes unpredictable and without real meaning.

The Tyrones themselves insistently refer their difficulties to defects of character, in the ceaseless arraignments entered by four judges at once too strict and too forgiving. But if characterological flaw is intrinsic to tragic drama, we should also be alert to the cultural environment in which the protagonists try to make their way. If they are guilty of being unrealistic, selfish, indulgent, wed to the addict's futile hunt for forgetfulness, may not that guilt be as much a function of the hazards imposed by their society as of their idiosyncratic weaknesses?

The Sick Family

Each of the Tyrones is ill, in varying modes of physical or psychological disability. The self-destructive pathologies that emerge in their efforts to cope with the problems of living form an array impressive in its scope and intensity: addiction, alcoholism, promiscuity, tuberculosis, arthritis. And undergirding the tangle of specific symptoms is the more pervasive sickness of being tired of life, paralyzed with revulsion against self and other and the society that bounds them. Their illnesses raise several questions. Why are they ill? Are they ill together, in a family neurosis or folie à quatre, or separately, or both? Contemporary studies of health and illness provide substantial evidence for the proposition that sickness of many kinds, including some that seems to be purely organic (like Edmund's tuberculosis), is very closely tied to the individual's total life circumstance. The damaged picture of the self that follows upon failed aspirations, the diminished self-esteem and feeling of incompetence, may be seen as a general causal factor in the Tyrones' maladaptation. Further, the life stress represented by expectable but threatening events, such as separation, the death of a family member, or job failure, has been shown to subject individuals to heightened risk of illness shortly after their occurrence. The individual syndromes of the Tyrones, perhaps most notably Mary's addiction, may also be traced to these types of unsettling happenings or "life-quakes." Thus the sicknesses that the family members assign to biological fate or moral insufficiency may be, in the light of current understanding, equally well or better explained by social and psychological causes. What haunts the Tyrones, as much as Irish ghosts or the shade of the Count of Monte Cristo, is the stress of living a life together.

The family pathology is here more than, or different from,

the mere enumeration or summing up of symptoms. Social psychiatrists are increasingly persuaded that neurotic behavior, like
healthy behavior, may be in large measure a process and product
of family interaction. Inadequate patterns of coping may be
communicated from one person to another or from one generation to another in a fashion as insidious as the contagion of
infectious disease. Thus Tyrone and Mary serve as destructive
exemplars for their sons, inducing in the boys their own grim
dance of high dreaming, of failed hope, of self-accusation and
accusation of others. And once underway, the habits of unhealthy
response are perpetuated; each member reinforces each other in
the downward spiral of hope without issue. The individual's
failure is mirrored in the failure of all. Thus Jamie cries when he
is forced to recognize that Mary is back on dope: "I suppose I
can't forgive her—yet. It meant so much. I'd begun to hope, if
she'd beaten the game, I could, too."[9]

Illness in modern populations tends to cluster and pile up in
certain groups. It is not spread at all evenly across a society. The
Tyrones are a model for the observation that sick families are
more ill than well families, and in more ways. The critical point
is that we are dealing with a deranged system and that the dis-
organization of the family group expresses itself in the plethora
of individual and shared symptoms.

The recurrent patterns of interaction in the Tyrone household may be analyzed in several ways. One might be termed the
quality or level of the interpersonal flow; another is the structure
of the relationships, the positioning of the characters in their
respective roles as family figures. The sociologist Erving Goffman,
in *The Presentation of Self in Everyday Life,* has written brilliantly
about the divers strategies individuals adopt in offering themselves to one another. O'Neill's people seem to "present" themselves on at least three interlaced levels, depending on situation
and mood.

The first is the level of conventional, prosaic interaction
that, as in all families and all human relationships of whatever
sort, serves to sustain the group in its pedestrian activities, its
"dailyness." This form meets the normal requirements of de-
cency and courtesy; it signals that they are members in a common humanity. (Here, the intercourse resembles that "phatic

communion'' I assign to Beckett's tramps in chapter 9.) The conventional mode also is important in that it protects the person from too close an examination of self and other. It might almost be described as a resting state, a matter-of-fact calm that precedes or follows the storms churned up by acute probing of others' motives or by the dangers of self-revelation.

A second level of discourse is exhibited in the volley of accusations directed each to each. The insistent drumfire of charges and countercharges is the play's dominant rhetorical theme. Members lay one another bare, and in mounting the several indictments or bills of particulars they display many of the old country–Irish features singled out by Raleigh: turbulence, obsession with betrayal, loquaciousness. Each of the Tryones believes he has been betrayed, and that if it were not for the perfidy of the other three members he might have fulfilled his promise. This candid, sometimes witty, often brutal level of interaction cannot be sustained indefinitely for two reasons. It threatens them, taxes them to nervous exhaustion, and if pressed to the limit, would destroy the family network on which each depends for his very identity even as he rails against it.

The mood of prosecutorial cynicism must also be relinquished on occasion for a more laudable reason than fear and anxiety—the very real love and affection the Tyrones hold for one another. This brings us to the third level of discourse, which might be characterized by the qualities of tenderness and concern. The characters probe more deeply than in the conventional level, but here they do so in an appreciative rather than a critical vein. Clearly, the long day's journey into hatred and disillusion is also a journey into love. The sin of indifference is not among the Tyrones' failings. They care very much, and the bitterness is the counterpart of the caring.

A significant feature of the family interplay, not unconnected with the need for and expression of love, is what might be termed the "strain toward normalcy." Despite all the tension and mutual recrimination, the Tyrones maintain something surprisingly close to a going concern. They strive to keep the ball in play, to match appropriate levels of discourse, to keep up, at a minimum, what one psychiatrist has called "pseudo-mutuality." In their patterned rehearsal of postures and words they seek equilibrium, each pushing the other just so far in accusation, then drawing back in alarm. All this indicates the normative strength of routine family roles, the effort to self-correct for deviance, the persistence of routine expectations. It might well be noted that certain currently fashionable demands for a fixed standard of candor and transparency in interpersonal relations (vulgarly phrased in such homilies as "telling it like it is" or "letting it all hang out") neglect that human beings cannot live always at the stretch or at high pitch. O'Neill does not make this mistake, and his drama gains verisimilitude from his aware- ness that some elements of customary evasion, omission, and mundane consensus are probably necessary for enduring rela- tionships. In one sense these steadying mechanisms, however hollowly they may at times ring, demonstrate the urge toward health, the way in which a small social system tries to compen- sate for disorder and to pull its members back toward some version of normalcy. The Tyrones prevail as a family not only because they have no alternative, but because they are con- cerned to preserve a fabric of civility, however rent.

Role positioning in this family represents virtually all the possible combinations involving four individuals. These pairings and coalitions include, significantly, one in which the four Tyrones are united as a team—the family against the world—as both center and boundary of its participants' lives. Internally, every three-to-one alliance is apparent, the remainder of the family arrayed against a single errant member. This form of alliance is most striking in the case of the three men poised against Mary; her illness and deviance are the most palpable, and Tyrone, Jamie, and Edmund coalesce to monitor her behavior, to discuss her condition behind her back, to try to keep her from her habit. Yet from time to time each individual finds the other three united in a script centering on his weaknesses: thus the shared image and shared concern for Tyrone's stinginess, for Jamie's alcoholism and promiscuity, for Edmund's illness and the dissipation that abets it. Each member is recurrently the target of scapegoating and stereotyping by a solid front of the other three. There are two other notable combinations in the Tyrone family game, an inter- generational split and a strong-weak split. Jamie and Edmund are brother conspirators, and they line up versus their parents to preserve their libertine dependence or to assert fresh artistic or philosophical values. Too, the sons exemplify the familiar pattern in acculturating families, the generational clash that occurs when the young have moved somewhat further toward the patterns of the host culture than have the old. Jamie and Tyrone are portrayed as fundamentally stronger than Mary and Edmund, especially in their vitality, physical health, and self-containedness. Hence father and older son comprise a pair who see themselves correctly as similar and who exercise vigilance toward the disabilities of Mary and Edmund. Jamie and Tyrone have the most searing brawls, but they unite in a protective stance toward the weaker pair.

The Revolt Against the Self

Katherine Hepburn is supposed to have remarked, during her performance as Mary in the film version of Long Day's Journey Into Night, that this was a play not about drug addiction but about people who have lost something. What have the Tyrones lost? I suggest they have lost their identities, their sense of the self as whole and worthy, and this is accompanied by, indeed inseparable from, the loss of a sense of family as community. For one's self-picture can only arise in, and be thereafter largely nourished by, the responses of those to whom one is importantly related. The picture each Tyrone forms of himself rests on the conceptions other family members hold; these conceptions are, as we have noted, ambiguous and confused but overwhelmingly negative. Not only has each failed to realize his ego ideal (as do all people), but his perception of a vast gulf between the ideal and the actual self is forever underlined by the rest of the family. So we find a collective failure of nerve, a vacuum of confidence, in which the individual's felt unworthiness is constantly thrown up at him and cruelly reinforced. Each too aware of his own weaknesses, the Tyrones are in full revolt against the self. The sounds that come through again and again in the play are the cries of the alienated self: self-contempt, self-deception, self-estrangement, self-pity. At length, both self and family are seen as prisons from which no escape is possible. The family past is the only important history, and it never lets go; the Tyrones seek a furtive relief in sensory derangement or brief physical flight or hollow fictions about an imagined future, but the relief is feeble and temporary.

The loss of identity is most pointedly expressed by Mary, speaking about Jamie but really about them all: "But I suppose life has made him like that, and he can't help it. None of us can help the things life has done to us. They're done before you realize it, and once they're done they make you do other things until at last everything comes between you and what you'd like to be, and you've lost your true self forever."[10] If the "true self" has been forever lost, the self that remains is somehow hateful and grotesque, to be condemned in forlorn expiation:

TYRONE: I wouldn't give a damn if you ever displayed the slightest sign of gratitude. The only thanks is to have you sneer at me for a dirty miser, sneer at my profession, sneer at every damned thing in the world—except yourself.

JAMIE: That's not true, Papa, You can't hear me talking to myself, that's all. . . .

EDMUND: . . . Who wants to see life as it is, if they can help it? It's the three Gorgons in one. You look in their faces and turn to stone. Or it's Pan. You see him and you die—that is, inside you—and have to go on living as a ghost.

TYRONE: . . . "We are such stuff as dreams are made on, and our little life is rounded with a sleep."

EDMUND: Fine! That's beautiful. But I wasn't trying to say that. We are such stuff as manure is made on, so let's drink up and forget it. That's more my idea.

· · ·

MARY: . . . How could you believe me—when I can't believe myself? I've become such a liar. I never lied about anything once upon a time. Now I have to lie, especially to myself. But how can you understand, when I don't myself. I've never understood anything about it, except that one day long ago I found I could no longer call my soul my own.[11]

In the end, perhaps *Long Day's Journey Into Night* is a drama about some universal losses in the modern world, as well as about the four Tyrones' specific losses: the loss of an innocent faith in an idealized self, the faith that the lonely individual can create through an act of will that self he would like to be; the loss of a sense of the family as guarantor of its members' authenticity, as final haven and repository for dreams of joy.

6

James Baldwin
Relationships of Love and Race

James Baldwin has asked the most urgent and penetrating questions any modern novelist has asked about certain key patterns of human relationships. Deeply thinking and deeply feeling, he explores the possibilities of love, the inevitabilities of hate, and the bloody angles of race relations. And these fearsome interrogations are carried out in the harsh, tangible realities of urban America. Further, Baldwin treats all these confrontations as the substance of the artist's essential task—to dig into himself and into others for truths about the human condition and to report the truths accurately and unflinchingly. He has much to tell us about the social roles and the psychological and sexual identities of men and women; he reveals the meanings of blackness and whiteness, and of their commingling, in the United States. His mastery of style renders his many sad truths not palatable but palpable; we feel them on the nerve. It also colors his few joyous truths with a luminous intensity, with a thrilling energy of awareness.

Black and White

Baldwin's great merit, the artist's merit, as a chronicler of race relations in America is that he makes us see and feel the subjective realities of the national torment. Behind the tracts and statistics, the histories and sociologies and psychologies, there are breathing people; Baldwin takes us into their minds and

hearts and forces upon us realizations that horrify and depress—
but that may ultimately heal. Particularly in his two best novels,
Go Tell It on the Mountain and *Another Country,* he examines
the interior sense of race and class, driving home the implications of these blunt facts of existence. He insists, first, on what we
might term the boundedness of lower-caste life, the relentless
feeling of entrapment and apprehension. Elizabeth, in *Go Tell It
on the Mountain,* recalls her early life in the city with Richard:

There was not, after all, a great difference between the world of the
North and that of the South which she had fled; there was only this
difference: the North promised more. And this similarity: what it promised it did not give, and what it gave, at length and grudgingly with one
hand, it took back with the other. Now she understood in this nervous,
hollow, ringing city, that nervousness of Richard's which had so attracted her—a tension so total, and so without the hope, or possibility of
release, or resolution, that she felt it in his muscles, and heard it in his
breathing, even as on her breast he fell asleep.[1]

This brief passage from "Elizabeth's Prayer" contains two other
quite characteristic Baldwin themes in addition to the trapped
tension—a view of the city, prototypically New York, as a coldly
hostile environment; and the recurrent comparison between the
North and the South in which neither region emerges as a society
at all promising for the black.

The idea of skin color as destiny, as not to be escaped by
whatever individual or group exertions, is the bedrock of the
black condition. It is expressed without compromise throughout
the novels, but perhaps never better than in a passage from
Another Country. Two whites, Vivaldo Moore and Cass Silenski,
are on their way to the funeral of Rufus Scott, a black musician
and friend to Vivaldo, who has taken his life in a plunge from the
George Washington Bridge. Vivaldo tells of his own cruel life as
a poor white in Brooklyn and of his love for Rufus:

He was crying, silently, and he bent forward, hiding his face with one
long hand. "I know I failed him, but I loved him, too, and nobody there
wanted to know that. I kept thinking, They're colored and I'm white but
the same things have happened, really the *same* things, and how can I
make them know that?"

"But they didn't," she said, "happen to you *because* you were
white. They just happened. But what happens up here"—and the cab

came out of the park; she stretched her hands, inviting him to look—"happens *because* they are colored. And that makes a difference." And, after a moment, she dared to add, "You'll be kissing a long time, my friend, before you kiss any of this away."[2]

Baldwin makes vivid the consequences of racial subordination for individual behavior and for the contours of black personality. His art might be almost a dramatization of the analysis of black psychological functioning set forth by the psychiatrists Abram Kardiner and Lionel Ovesey in their provocative study *The Mark of Oppression*. They argue that the "mark" imposed by the long history of discrimination and enforced inequality contains the central elements of low self-esteem and aggression. Attempts to deal with these elements are a series of largely futile maneuvers, self-defeating in the main, as long as the social structure of injustice remains in place. Although the years since Kardiner and Ovesey's research and since the first publication of Baldwin's novels have been distinguished by some very important charges in educational and occupational opportunity and by the abolition of legal segregation, the damage and rage are still with us in significant quantities. Baldwin captures them as no other writer, black or white, has ever done.

Rufus Scott may best be seen as the hero of *Another Country*. Despite the fact that his suicide occurs early in the novel, his life has been the focal point for the other actors of both races, and his memory remains, obsessively, at their center of attention. Rufus is a superbly drawn exemplar of the failure of self-esteem in the oppressed, and of the virulent aggression that must in the end—lacking other outlets—be turned inward against the self. We meet him as a gifted young musician, a drummer, friended by members of both races, self-assured and promising. He leaves us, after an abortive affair with a southern white girl and a seeming failure of nerve in his art and his life, as an embittered down-and-outer without hope. What has happened to Rufus, what steers him toward his lonely leap into the cold Hudson River? It is precisely a constantly diminished self-esteem, an inability to respect himself under the battering of a hostile society that sees him as black and worthless, precisely a failure to handle his aggression, to control the rage that leads him to beat and scorn his lover, Leona, and at length to destroy himself. Few cries of rage can match Rufus's toward the end of his rope.

"How I hate them—all those white sons of bitches out there. They're trying to kill me, you think I don't know? They got the world on a string, man, the miserable white cock suckers, and they tying that string around my neck, they killing *me*." He turned into the room again; he did not look at Vivaldo. "Sometimes I lie here and I listen—just listen. They out there, scuffling, making that change, they think it's going to last forever. Sometimes I lie here and listen, listen for a bomb, man, to fall on this city and make all that noise stop. I listen to hear them moan, I want them to bleed and choke, I want to hear them *crying*, man, for somebody to come help them. They'll cry a long time before *I* come down there. . . . "You got to fight with the landlord because the landlord's *white*! You got to fight with the elevator boy because the motherfucker's *white*. Any bum on the Bowery can shit all over you because maybe he can't hear, can't see, can't walk, can't fuck—but he's *white*!"[3]

The aggression of black against white is no more terrifying than the aggression of black against black, and of course, the roots of the latter are similar. Self-hate is easily generalized to others caught in the same caste predicament; they mirror the diminished self. And they are also, in some sense, safe targets for anger deflected from its true targets—the whites. In *Go Tell It on the Mountain*, Baldwin presents a black world in which white society is rarely an explicit part of the action. The white majority is here rather a brooding, menacing presence, ever threatening and framing the strict limits of the habitable social universe. In the South, as in Harlem, the black community waits in silent fear.

On that day, a day he was never to forget, he went when work was done to buy some medicine for Deborah, who was in bed with a misery in her back. Night had not yet fallen and the streets were gray and empty— save that here and there, polished in the light that spilled outward from a poolroom or a tavern, white men stood in groups of half a dozen. As he passed each group, silence fell, and they watched him insolently, itching to kill; but he said nothing, bowing his head, and they knew, anyway, that he was a preacher. There were no black men on the streets at all, save him. There had been found that morning, just outside of town, the dead body of a soldier, his uniform shredded where he had been flogged, and, turned upward through the black skin, raw, red meat. . . . Now, someone spat on the sidewalk at Gabriel's feet, and he walked on, his face not changing, and he heard it reprovingly whispered behind him that he was a good nigger, surely up to no trouble. He hoped that he would not be spoken to, that he would not have to smile into any of these so well-known white faces. While he walked, held by his caution more rigid than an arrow, he prayed, as his mother had taught him to pray, for loving kindness; yet he dreamed of the feel of a white man's forehead against his shoe; again and again, until the head wobbled on the broken neck and his foot encountered nothing but the rushing blood.[4]

But Gabriel, like other blacks in the story, cannot realize his dream of direct retaliation. His anger turns fiercely inward, in the orgiastic self-scourging of fundamentalist religion, and as fiercely outward, to the wives and sisters and sons who cannot in any way please him. *Go Tell It on the Mountain* is a remarkable evocation of a closed, narrow caste world. Its characters, drenched in primitive Christianity, can yet afford no tenderness or affection for one another. Their flamboyant, nearly savage religious life serves several purposes; in it may be seen once again the twin themes of low self-esteem and plentiful aggression. The root assumption of incorrigible human sinfulness provides justification for a portrait of black self and other as unworthy and doomed. Here the Gospel reinforces and sustains the underdog role by construing all men as underdogs in a wicked world whose shape and inhabitants cannot be bettered by merely human effort. Abundant rage is directed at the worthless self and at one's kin, who are equally damned. A fierce, unforgiving God supplants and supplements the malevolent white society without. Too, the very vocal and physical rites, the turbulent and frenzied atmosphere of the church, provide an emotional release that is everywhere else forbidden. In a hard life that is not susceptible to improvement, religion holds out the last hope it has always held out for those on the social bottom—a life to come.

Black anger against blacks is pervasive in the novel. Thus the narrator, the boy John, nourishes his resentment of his preacher father, Gabriel:

This was not, in John, a faith subject to death or alteration, nor yet a hope subject to destruction; it was his identity, and part, therefore, of that wickedness for which his father beat him and to which he clung in order to withstand his father. His father's arm, rising and falling, might make him cry, and that voice might cause him to tremble; yet his father could never be entirely the victor, for John cherished something that his father could not reach. It was his hatred and his intelligence that he cherished, the one feeding the other. He lived for the day when his father would be dying and he, John, would curse him on his deathbed.[5]

And so Gabriel's sister, Florence, falls to pray and hate simultaneously:

She knew that Gabriel rejoiced, not that her humility might lead her to grace, but only that some private anguish had brought her low: her song revealed that she was suffering, and this her brother was glad to see. This had always been his spirit. Nothing had ever changed it; nothing ever would. For a moment her pride stood up; the resolution that had brought her to this place tonight faltered, and she felt that if Gabriel was the Lord's anointed, she would rather die and endure Hell for all eternity than bow before His altar.[8]

Alexander H. Leighton, in an effort to sum up the minimum needs of the individual, sets forth ten "striving sentiments."[7] All men, he contends, strive for at least these basic satisfactions, and a prolonged failure to experience them may generate psychological disorder. If we simply enumerate the strivings, the barest of comments will make plain how the black condition implies their systematic frustration.

Physical security—Historically, of course, this has been a continuing black problem in terms both of economic sufficiency and sheer physical safety. This is ever-present in Baldwin, especially when he deals with the lower-class milieu of *Go Tell It on the Mountain*.

Sexual expression—Here the novelist shows an interesting ambivalence: black sexual behavior is seen as rich and intense, but in certain ways ultimately unsatisfying. The barriers to fulfillment are at least two. In the atmosphere of fundamentalist religion, sexual release is, although necessary, sinful and dirty. For the black liberated from this religion, such as many of the characters in *Another Country*, sex tends to be viewed in terms of exploitation, and the sexual life is tainted by the lack of self-esteem.

Expressing and receiving love—The wounded, distorted self-picture that is a consequence of caste oppression militates against the possibilities of lovingness. Affectionate relationships are at the core of Baldwin's concern, and we shall examine them more fully below. Basically, as the characters demonstrate, the absence of self-respect and self-trust works against openness; unable to accept the self comfortably, Baldwin's men and women find it hard to accept the other. Each is unable to believe himself worthy of another's love, and the long history of betrayal of black hopes makes the deep trusting of love very unlikely.

Expressing hostility—In the black experience, as noted earlier, aggression cannot safely be directed at the real source of frustration, the white community. Hence, it is insistently forced inward, as in the masochistic career of Rufus Scott, or toward fellow blacks, as in the tortured interplay of kin in *Go Tell It on the Mountain*.

Securing recognition—Again it is clear that traditionally the avenues for recognition have been few and foreshortened for blacks. In the contemporary United States, of course, recognition accrues preëminently from occupational attainment. Baldwin illustrates the impoverished structure of opportunity by describing his black protagonists as holding menial or musical jobs. Thus Rufus's sister, Ida, in *Another Country*, works as a waitress while trying to become a singer; Rufus, when he works at all, is a drummer. All of the characters in the earlier novel are menials who can seek shreds of recognition only in the narrow confines of the fundamentalist church.

Exercising volition—This striving is variously phrased as being creative or exerting a positive force on one's environment. Few outlets are typically available in the powerless black world of the novels. The individual is overwhelmingly subject to the volition of the white majority. Again, culturally induced low self-esteem renders genuine volition problematic; assurance, self-confidence, a history of past success—all these supports of a mastering orientation toward the social world are in perilously short supply.

Orientation to one's place in society, and to the places of others—It might be said that blacks in Baldwin's view have in one sense all too firm a conception of their "place" in society—

grimly and inalterably at the bottom. But this knowledge affords neither solace nor security in a caste structure so little amenable to change. Baldwin underlines how the traditional bondage of blackness in the South is exchanged in the flight north for the ambiguities and tensions of the city.

Group membership—As in the foregoing sentiment, group membership for the Black is at once too rigid and too fragile. In *Go Tell It on the Mountain* the only available group anchorage is a suffocating primitive religion. The people who live in *Another Country* are essentially without group supports; their networks have been ripped apart by the impersonality of the city. Blacks here must seek membership in the tenuous, racially mixed friendship of artistic groups, or fall back on the spare and conflict-ridden resources of the ghetto.

Being in and of a moral order—This sentiment implies a felt sense of rightness in conduct and adherence to a stable core of shared values. Once more the two novels sketch a contrast: the individual can be part of a fixed moral order if he gives himself over to the demanding strictures of the religious congregation, but this is a bleak and forbidding fixity that literally drowns the person; or, cast loose in the hellish New York of *Another Country*, he can contrive to mint a fresh, personalized moral order that requires immense resources of nerve and sensitivity. In either case the sentiment is exceedingly difficult to fulfill.

We have, then, looked at two conceptualizations of black personality and interpersonal relations under the stress of caste. James Baldwin's art makes them come alive, and they in turn may contribute to our fuller understanding of his fictional achievement. The wicked angularities of race relations may be summed up by two cries from the brother and sister of *Another Country*. Ida Scott gazes at Seventh Avenue.

"But, Cass, ask yourself, look out and ask yourself—wouldn't you hate all white people if they kept you in prison here?" They were rolling up startling Seventh Avenue. The entire population seemed to be in the streets, draped, almost, from lamp posts, stoops, and hydrants, and walking through the traffic as though it were not there. "Kept you here, and stunted you and starved you, and made you watch your mother and father and sister and lover and brother and son and daughter die or go mad or go under, before your very eyes? And not in a hurry, like from one day to the next, but, every day, every day, for years, for generations? Shit. They keep you here because you're black, the filthy, white cock suckers, while they go around jerking themselves off with all that jazz about the land of the free and the home of the brave. And they want you to jerk yourself off with that same music, too, only, keep your distance. Some days, honey, I wish I could turn myself into one big fist and grind this country to powder. Some days, I don't believe it has a right to exist."[8]

Her brother Rufus, closely observant even as he perishes, surveys his fellows during his last subway ride: "At Fifty-ninth Street many came on board and many rushed across the platform to the waiting local. Many white people and many black people, chained together in time and in space, and by history, and all of them in a hurry. In a hurry to get away from each other, he thought, but we ain't never going to make it. We been fucked for fair."[9]

Modalities of Love

If black and white can truly never get away from each other, especially in the urban sink of Manhattan and other great cities, then they must somehow live together. The terms of coexistence, now frightening, now brimming with a strange joy, are relentlessly explored in Baldwin's novels. He limns the rights and obligations of love in its manifold guises.

As an acute questioner of how we can love one another, Baldwin ranges over a wide landscape of relatedness: male-female; black-white; black-black; male-male. Each of the pairings is convincing in its tenderness and fierceness, in its potential for elation and disappointment. In *Another Country* we seem to be light years away from the simplicities and certitudes of love in a Hemingway or a Fitzgerald. Without illusion, embittered by past defeats, Baldwin's people yet make huge demands on one another's capacity for loving. They rip and tear and curse at each other, they cry and laugh, they probe for the fullest revelation and acceptance. Profoundly lonely, they seek to drown in the other; drowning, they summon an angry pride in reasserting their individuality. Love, and particularly sexual love, is for Baldwin the final test of the person's authenticity. Love, analogous to and part of creativity itself, also represents man's ultimate goal, a consummation of life lived at the highest pitch.

The modalities of love in the novelist's world are all adventurous; they entail risk, danger, the courage to embark on a journey whose end is not and never can be in sight. Self-surrender is at once sought and feared. The demands of loving, on both the self and the other, are so overwhelming that the characters break under the weight, as Rufus Scott does, or survive in a fragile and precarious balance. Nothing is ever settled; everything is always in process, in the endless discovery and testing of one's humanness and integrity. The parallels between love and artistic creativity, although seldom made explicit, sound an insistent undertone in Baldwin's work. Both require a strict honesty toward experience, a willingness to lose the self at least temporarily, a boldness of naïve engagement. The sexual act and the artist's act share many features; the kinship of the words "creation" and "procreation" is not at all fortuitous.

Love's torment and pain, and its exhilaration, are struck at once in *Another Country* in the first encounter between Rufus and Leona. Having picked one another up in the club where Rufus is playing, they come together on their host's balcony at an after-hours party:

And she carried him, as the sea will carry a boat: with a slow, rocking and rising and falling motion, barely suggestive of the violence of the deep. They murmured and sobbed on this journey, he softly, insistently cursed. Each labored to reach a harbor: there could be no rest until this motion became unbearably accelerated by the power that was rising in them both. Rufus opened his eyes for a moment and watched her face, which was transfigured with agony and gleamed in the darkness like alabaster. Tears hung in the corners of her eyes and the hair at her brow was wet. Her breath came with moaning and short cries, with words he couldn't understand, and in spite of himself he began moving faster and thrusting deeper. He wanted her to remember him the longest day she lived. And shortly, nothing could have stopped him, not the white God himself nor a lynch mob arriving on wings. Under his breath he cursed the milk-white bitch and groaned and rode his weapon between her thighs.[10]

Rufus loves Leona, and she gives herself entirely to him. But his hatred of her whiteness and his self-contempt for his own blackness poison their relationship; at length both are destroyed by the attempt to love. Nor has Rufus been conspicuously more successful in his long friendship with the white writer, Vivaldo, or his homosexual affair with the white actor, Eric. Each of these whites may be said to love Rufus; the depth of their caring is exceeded only by that of his sister, Ida. Yet Rufus, unable to accept himself, is finally unable to accept others. He must lash out, must ceaselessly question the validity of others' commitment to him, must compulsively act in ways that repel his friends and lovers and confirm him in his self-derogation.

The abundance of sexual coalitions and conflicts in *Another Country* is an effective counterpoint to Baldwin's focus on race relations. He asks not only whether black can love white, but basically whether any two human beings can submerge their selfishness and brittle egos in a profound realization of each other. His people, all articulate, find the communication of their real thoughts and feelings a difficult and ever unfinished challenge. They are in a social environment—the Western urban world—that offers few sure guides to conduct. And they have rejected traditional concepts of male and female roles, just as they have rejected the conventional sexual isolation of black from white or of male from male. And so they search for alliances, some brief and some prolonged, that will yield them at once a sense of self and the security of being in and of another.

Vivaldo and Ida form the couple around whom the novel's action revolves. They face the interwoven hazards of race and sex with exuberance, with self-doubt and jealous awareness, and with a seemingly durable affection and mutual need. Their physical passion, joyous and believable, is surrounded by the fact of color; their love, whether harshly urgent or domestically placid, is gnawed by an apprehension of the ultimate unknowability or impenetrability of another's person. Vivaldo wonders about their future together:

They would learn everything about each other, they had time, she would tell him. Would she? Or would she merely accept his secrets as she accepted his body, happy to be the vehicle of his relief? While offering in return (for she knew the rules) revelations intended to pacify and also intended to frustrate him; to frustrate, that is, any attempt on his part to strike deeper into that incredible country in which, like the princess of fairy tales, sealed in a high tower and guarded by beasts, bewitched and exiled, she paced her secret round of secret days.[11]

Much later, after they have lived together in the city, Vivaldo's doubts still assert themselves: "Perhaps she loved him, perhaps she did: but if she did, how was it, then, that they remained so locked away from one another? Perhaps it was he who did not know how to give, did not know how to love. Love was a country he knew nothing about."[12] Love is here indeed a mystery, "another country"; but it is a terrain Baldwin's characters explore with intelligence and nerve.

Baldwin is one of the very few artists who have been able to write convincingly about homosexual love; he renders both the affection and the physical expression somehow natural and inevitable. Perhaps not since the Thomas Mann of *Death in Venice* has the tender love of men for one another been so effectively portrayed. Much like the love between black and white, the love between men is perilous; it is exposed to the scorn of the heterosexual majority, much as black-white pairings draw the hostility of both races. Baldwin, nevertheless, suggests that the imperatives and capacities of lovingness remain as a constant in human relationships. What his men seek and find in one another is not psychologically different from the "normal" interplay between men and women. In *Another Country* the love between Eric and his French companion, the boy Yves, entails all the openness and commitment, the sense of vulnerability and the hope of refuge, that characterize any intimate coming together. The novelist instructs us on the necessary danger of relinquishing the surface self, the defensive mask, in the service of a deeper searching and mutual affirmation of selfhood. Eric recalls earlier affairs: "When the liaison so casually begun survived the first encounters, when a kind of shy affection began to force itself up through the frozen ground, and shame abated, chaos more than ever ruled. For shame had not so much abated as found a partner. Affection had appeared, but through a fissure, a crevice, in the person, through which, behind affection, came all the winds of fear. For the act of love is a confession. One lies about the body but the body does not lie about itself; it cannot lie about the force which drives it."[13] He then recounts the tension of his first meeting with Yves, when they have not yet approached the edge of discovery of themselves as lovers.

Eric chattered on, delighted by Yves's changing face, waiting for his smile, waiting for his laugh. He wanted Yves to know that he was not trying to strike with him the common, brutal bargain; was not buying him a dinner in order to throw him into bed. And by and by this unspoken declaration caused Yves to nod gravely, as though he were turning it over in his mind. There also appeared in his face a certain fear. It was this fear which Eric sometimes despaired of conquering, in Yves, or in himself. It was the fear of making a total commitment, a vow: it was the fear of being loved.[14]

The commitment is made; Yves and Eric are tender partners, responsive and playful. Eric will make love to others in the city, to Cass and Vivaldo, but his tie to Yves endures.

At length, Baldwin insists that although love is a strange, alien world, frightening and demanding, it is the only country worth having. The infinitely lonely prison of the locked-up self is the sole alternative, and it is not to be sustained. His lovers gamble their very lives. They are exposed. As Cass reflects to herself, "And terrifying that the terms of love are so rigorous, its checks and liberties so tightly bound together."[15] But in the gamble, in living on these rigorous terms, lies the possibility of becoming fully alive, fully human. In this high seeking lies, also, the one promise—bright and rich, if inevitably transitory—of a safe harbor for the isolated individual in the pounding seas of this century.

The Urban Sink

Researchers on the activities of laboratory animals under conditions of extreme overcrowding report a situation they describe as a "behavioral sink." Frenzied and frustrated by crowding, Norway rats leave their usual patterns of action and enter into chaotic, self-defeating behaviors: they kill one another aimlessly, devour their young, become sexually impotent. Baldwin's image of the city in *Another Country* might fairly be termed "the urban sink." Although he expresses the restless power and artificial glitter of New York and the nervous vitality of the artist in the city, his vision is basically fixed on its dehumanizing properties.

The city is a cold, dirty, hostile arena; its architecture looms over the people, a brooding presence, like some great beast snuffing out energy and hope. Individuals frantically brush past one another in a gray, bleak, ugly atmosphere, and where they come together or have been together an acrid stench settles. Each person is lost, and many are crucified in this so familiar but so foreign land. The city emerges not just as the stage for the tortures of love and caste and class, but as itself a malevolent force that intrudes and repels, that bounds the possibilities of life. We see blacks with the juices beaten out—and whites with the juices drained out.

The model of the metropolis advanced by early sociologists, notably Georg Simmel and Louis Wirth, emphasized the city's impersonality, its plethora of "secondary" relationships in which individuals enact specialized, fragmented roles rather than engaging as full human partners, its domination by money and markets at the expense of any other measures of human worthfulness. As Simmel writes: "The deepest problems of modern life derive from the claim of the individual to preserve the autonomy and individuality of his existence in the face of overwhelming social forces, of historical heritage, of external culture, and of the technique of life."[16] Critics of this model counter that rural and small town life may be quite as stifling and barren; they point out the opportunities the city affords for variety, discourse, creative ferment. Baldwin does not deny the excitement of New York, and he holds no romantic conception of pastoral harmony and delight. But the places where most of his people can afford to live and the work they are able or are allowed to do do not permit them to master the urban environment. They are dominated by the city as a trap from which there is no flight. Rufus Scott is killed by many things working in concert to bring him down, and the physical city stands for them.

The great buildings, unlit, blunt like the phallus or sharp like the spear, guarded the city which never slept.

Beneath them Rufus walked, one of the fallen—for the weight of this city was murderous—one of those who had been crushed on the day, which was every day, these towers fell. Entirely alone, and dying of it, he was part of an unprecedented multitude. There were boys and girls drinking coffee at the drugstore counters who were held back from his condition by barriers as perishable as their dwindling cigarettes. They could scarcely bear their knowledge, nor could they have borne the sight of Rufus, but they knew why he was in the streets tonight, why he rode subways all night long, why his stomach growled, why his hair was nappy, his armpits funky, his pants and shoes too thin, and why he did not dare to stop and take a leak.[17]

And even if one is not in Rufus's extremity, is not down and out with failed nerve, the city is a steady oppressor. Consider Eric's New York:

And the summer came, the New York summer, which is like no summer anywhere. The heat and the noise began their destruction of nerves and sanity and private lives and love affairs. . . . It was a city without oases, run entirely, insofar, at least, as human perception could tell, for money; and its citizens seemed to have lost entirely any sense of their right to renew themselves. Whoever, in New York, attempted to cling to this right, lived in New York in exile—in exile from the life around him; and this, paradoxically, had the effect of placing him in perpetual danger of being forever banished from any real sense of himself.[18]

The Writer's Work

Baldwin has the courage to search both his blackness and his homosexuality, to rake and scourge his own experience. Only in this fashion can he penetrate what caste membership means, what certain forms of human loving entail, what living in the urban sink implies. This exquisite self-probing, painful and revelatory, leads him then to universal observations about the quest for the self and the strict demands of full interpersonal engagement. Above all, he places on each human being the charge placed upon the artist: to be deeply honest, to avoid easy answers, to be the opposite of complacent.

Baldwin says the most complete reexperiencing of the individual's history is the prerequisite for self-knowledge as it is for creative effort. But if this total emotional reliving is the key to personal and artistic authenticity, as Proust exemplifies and psychoanalysis affirms, it is also a perilous journey for even the strongest among us. In *Another Country* we are shown two novelists at work; one, Vivaldo, is still open, if unfulfilled—he may make it through, although he has not yet; the other, Richard Silenski, has compromised himself in a milder and safer achievement. Cass muses on Vivaldo's failure to recapture the past and Richard's unwitting renunciation of it:

No. It was not expressed. She wondered why. Perhaps it was because Vivaldo's recollections in no sense freed him from the things recalled. He had not gone back into it—that time, that boy; he regarded it with a fascinated, even romantic horror, and he was looking for a way to deny it.

Perhaps such secrets, the secrets of everyone, were only expressed when the person laboriously dragged them into the light of the world, imposed them on the world, and made them a part of the world's experience. Without this effort, the secret place was merely a dungeon in which the person perished; habitable darkness; and she saw, with a dreadful reluctance, why this effort was so rare. Reluctantly, because she then realized that Richard had bitterly disappointed her by writing a book in which he did not believe. In that moment she knew, and she knew that Richard would never face it, that the book he had written to make money represented the absolute limit of his talent. It had not really been written to make money—if only it had been! It had been written because he was afraid, afraid of things dark, strange, dangerous, difficult, and deep.[19]

Baldwin's merit is that he has made the rare effort and has thrown a white light on "the secrets of everyone."

7

Boris Pasternak

Ideology and Privacy

Pasternak's *Doctor Zhivago* stands firmly in the classic tradition of the Russian novel. Like its great nineteenth-century predecessors, it is dense, vivid, sprawling—a many-peopled canvas. Like them, too, it addresses the large moral questions that frame interpersonal conduct; in particular, the novel probes that calculus of rights and duties that is fundamental to our conceptions of social roles, asking what we owe to others and to ourselves. But despite Pasternak's adherence to the traditional form and the faintly old-fashioned flavor of his descriptive amplitude, he is marvelously contemporary in posing the issues facing modern man in an age of overarching polities, elaborate social organization, and demands for ideological allegiance. *Doctor Zhivago* is a story of love in the chaotic welter of social revolution; it is also a remarkable evocation of the contest between the abstract and the concrete in giving direction to human affairs. Perhaps most important, Pasternak's imaginative achievement is grounded in the search for the private and the individual in a society (and not only the USSR) increasingly dedicated to a public definition of experience.

Pasternak is at one with Camus, and with the earlier questioners Ibsen and Shaw, in urging that men and women constantly reassess the values by which they live. He is as much an antiidealist as Ibsen in his message that the individual must persist in testing and refining his ideals in the light of immediate experience. He is as much the rebel as Camus in refusing to sacrifice the person on the abstract but massively powerful altars of history or ideology or the nation state. *Doctor Zhivago* is a profound expression of Shaw's "quintessence of Ibsenism": "In short, our ideals, like the gods of old, are constantly demanding human sacrifices. Let none of them, says Ibsen, be placed above the obligation to prove itself worth the sacrifices it demands; and let everyone religiously refuse to sacrifice himself and others from the moment he loses his faith in the validity of the ideal. . . . What Ibsen insists on is that there is no golden rule; that conduct must justify itself by its effect upon life and not by its conformity to any rule or ideal."[1]

Yurii Zhivago and his lover Lara cannot staunch the thirst to question the ideals of the emerging socialist state and of the approved revolutionary modes of conduct. Because they are Ibsenites in a totalitarian climate, they cannot survive. Because he had created them and let them take their true course, faithful to themselves, Pasternak was unable to accept the Nobel Prize and unable to enjoy a Russian audience for his masterwork.

The Artist under Totalitarianism

Pasternak and his fictional hero Zhivago comprise a double image of the artist's condition in an atmosphere of "socialist realism" and repressive cultural vigilance. As Zhivago the poet resists the revolution and is crushed by it, so Pasternak resists the official Soviet literary policy and dies little honored and exiled in his own country. Pasternak's is a classic case history of one type of artistic career in a highly organized authoritarian society— the rebellious artist who is unable or unwilling to abide by the doctrines set forth as official ideology and who refuses to portray the life of his times in a manner approved by the cultural guardians of the state.

At least since Plato, of course, philosophers of the well-ordered state have sensed the danger to received values represented by the poet. Thus in the well-known passage from *The Republic*, Plato argues against the "honeyed muse": "But we must remain firm in our conviction that hymns to the gods and praises of famous men are the only poetry which ought to be admitted into our State. For if you go beyond this and allow the honeyed muse to enter, either in epic or lyric verse, not law and the reason of mankind, which by common consent have ever been deemed best, but pleasure and pain will be the rulers in our State."[2]

Pasternak and Zhivago embody the tragic sense of life. For them, pleasure and pain distinguish man's relation to man, and this primary interplay transcends in importance the fearful symmetry of governmental apparatus. The Platonic view, which is essentially the view of the arts adopted by modern totalitarian polities, rests on two key assumptions. The first is that social order can be achieved only under a unified, monolithic code of value. The durability of the Western democracies under valuative and artistic pluralism seems to argue against this premise, although one might contend that in the long sweep of history the jury is still out. The second postulate is that in some fashion the arts are significant in shaping the behavior of their audiences. Clearly, the poet is no danger unless one assumes that he is listened to and that his hearers act differently thereafter. There is little evidence to support this assumption, although lovers of the arts feel it in their hearts to be true. It appears most probable that the efficacy of poetry and the other arts in influencing social action is subtle, indirect, and slow, occuring through the reshaping of language and hence of perceptual alternatives. The direct translation of literature into political action seems hardly possible. In any event, the ideologues of the Soviet state accept both assumptions. Having done so, they must necessarily take art so seriously that the censorship and repression experienced by Pasternak, by Solzhenitsyn currently, and by a long line of artistic martyrs inevitably follow.

The note sounds emphatically in Leon Trotsky's *Literature and Revolution* and continues essentially unbroken to the present time, despite the "freezes" and "thaws" in the severity with which artistic dogma is enforced. Trotsky announces the high seriousness of art, remarking that "the development of art is the highest test of the vitality and significance of each epoch." But at length, although Trotsky's discussion is more sophisticated and sympathetic toward the arts than the actions of many of his heirs in cultural surveillance would suggest, he concludes: "We ought to have a watchful revolutionary censorship. . . . If the Revolution has the right to destroy bridges and art monuments whenever necessary, it will stop still less from laying its hand on any tendency in art which, no matter how great its achievement in form, threatens to disintegrate the revolutionary environment or to arouse the internal forces of the Revolution, that is, the proletariat, the peasantry and the intelligentsia, to a hostile opposition to one another."[3]

Yurii Zhivago's environment is substantially different from his creator's. In the chaos of war and revolution, the organized cultural commissariat is not yet in place. But the fundamental themes are already apparent, and Zhivago, the prescient poet, is sensible to them and finds them repugnant. He has embraced the ideals of the revolution in his youth; loving the grace notes of upper-middle-class life-style, he is nevertheless alert to the hateful and the oppressive features of Czarist Russia. His disillusion is therefore the more poignant. His is the poet's cry for individuality and creativity:

But, first, the idea of social betterment as it is understood since the October revolution doesn't fill me with enthusiasm. Second, it is so far from being put into practice, and the mere talk about it has cost such a sea of blood, that I'm not sure that the end justifies the means. And last—and this is the main thing—when I hear people speak of reshaping life it makes me lose my self-control and I fall into despair. . . . Reshaping life! People who can say that have never understood a thing about life—they have never felt its breath, its heartbeat—however much they have seen or done. They look on it as a lump of raw material that needs to be processed by them, to be ennobled by their touch. But life is never a material, a substance to be molded. If you want to know, life is the principle of self-renewal, it is constantly renewing and remaking and changing and transfiguring itself, it is infinitely beyond your or my obtuse theories about it.[4]

Yurii rails against the planned society and the "obtuse theories" of socialist ideology. His lover, Lara, complements this defiance by speaking for autonomy, for individual value judgments: "It was then that untruth came down on our land of Russia. The main misfortune, the root of all the evil to come, was the loss of confidence in the value of one's own opinion. People imagined that it was out of date to follow their own moral sense, that they must all sing in chorus, and live by other people's notions,

notions that were being crammed down everybody's throat."[5] All too understandably, these are hardly sentiments that can be sanctioned for publication in the Soviet Union.

Pasternak and his hero exemplify a bitter and fascinating paradox in the role of the artist in society: where he is taken most seriously, he is least free; where his art is regarded as basically frivolous, where society views him, in Mark Twain's telling phrase, as "not connected to the works," he is most at liberty to create what he will.

This contrast between the almost casual freedom of the poet in the Western democracies and the hemmed-in but respected role of the Soviet writer is further underlined by the Polish poet, Czeslaw Milosz: "Fear of the indifference with which the economic system of the West treats its artists and scholars is widespread among Eastern intellectuals. They say it is better to deal with an intelligent devil than with a good-natured idiot. An intelligent devil understands their mutual interests and lets them live by a pen, a chisel, or a brush, caring for his clients and making his demands. A good-natured idiot does not understand these interests, gives nothing and asks nothing—which in practice amounts to polite cruelty."[6]

Pasternak's life offers us a quite different version of the vicissitudes of the writer's career than we have seen in the lives of Western artists such as Fitzgerald or O'Neill or Hemingway. He confronted a state that was vitally interested in literature; they were allowed to go their own way, beset by economic uncertainty and the vagaries of popular and critical taste. He suffered censorship but was confirmed in a significant social role; they were exposed to the strains of an exquisite freedom, to the imperatives of carving out and enunciating a role for themselves. Yet I think it would be in some ways a mistake to overdraw the contrasts. Ultimately, whatever the formal governmental and ideological climate in which the poet lives, he is concerned, in Frank Kermode's term, with "making sense of our lives." If there are sharp distinctions in the degree of creative freedom he is vouchsafed and in the weight his role is assigned by his society, there are still more important constants. Always and everywhere, the writer's imaginative labor is focused on clarifying the language of experience, on presenting us with alternative shapes for the conduct of our behavior toward nature, toward one another, and toward our inner selves.

"The Whirlpool's Shrieking Face"

Dante Gabriel Rossetti, in his poem *Jenny*, describes the heroine as a "poor handful of bright spring water, flung in the whirlpool's shrieking face." The image may be taken as a motif for the fates of the men and women in *Doctor Zhivago*. For Pasternak shows us what might be called the microcosm of revolution—the infinite disruption and intimate turbulence of individual lives under the impress of vast, precarious social change. The onrush of events is so furious, the scope of change in values and life-styles so sweeping, that the individual comes to feel himself powerless, adrift, with no steady anchor for his concepts of self or of the roles of others. Even the strongest person, and Zhivago is in some ways very resilient, can be made distraught and confused by whelming change: "[Yurii] realized that he was a pygmy before the monstrous machine of the future; he was anxious about this future, and loved it and was secretly proud of it, and as though for the last time, as if in farewell, he avidly looked at the trees and clouds and the people walking in the streets, and the great Russian city struggling through misfortune—and was ready to sacrifice himself for the general good, and could do nothing."[7]

The acute derangement of Zhivago's family life, his professional and artistic roles, his personal morale—all these are emblems of the sensitive individual exposed to chaotic change. As happens so often in literature, Pasternak, the perceptive artist, grasps intuitively certain of the most important aspects of the social psychological study of change. We see the potential consequences of these pervasive dislocations for individual physical and mental health and for the stability of social relationships, and for the sense of community or shared values. Zhivago experiences a set of life events that is nearly a formula for inspiring the deterioration that steadily overtakes him.

Recent research in social psychiatry and kindred fields has supplied rather convincing evidence that the kind of life-quakes fostered by revolution are strongly associated with increased risk to the health of the exposed person. Zhivago is battered by all combinations of deleterious stress: intermittent or prolonged separation from significant persons; lack of opportunity to practice his medical vocation or his literary avocation; material deprivation; isolation; acute uncertainty about the demands of his environment and his capacity to master them. And so we find him reeling through life, suffering from infectious disease, fatigue, progressive heart disease, and an unsureness about his proper work and proper love. Combined, they lead to his spiraling demoralization and early death. As Svetlana Alliluyeva writes in her affecting tribute:

Dear, dear Yurii Andreyevich, this gifted and humble doctor whose name comes from the word for "life," from the word for everything living— "Zhivago" in Church Slavic. . . . How he suffers, this gifted and hardworking man, at the hollow sound of empty words divorced from the realities of life! . . . Yes, he had a magical command of words, he wrote poetry, he healed the sick, he loved the daily round of life in all its fullness and vigor, he shunned no work, however menial, he was a true aristocrat of the spirit, he labored for the good of his fellow men. And there was no place for him in a society that demanded of him service to the dead letter instead of work and the single-minded exercise of his creative powers. Small wonder that he found himself an outcast, doomed slowly to sink lower and lower.[8]

The Poet and Organized Society

Svetlana Alliluyeva's references to "the hollow sound of empty words" and "service to the dead letter" go to the root of one of the vital conflicts between Zhivago and Soviet society— and, by implication, to a conflict between any artist and a highly organized polity or an officially phrased ideology. Zhivago as imagined poet and Pasternak as his creator confront the formal repression of totalitarianism and the chaos of civil war and revolution. But on a deeper level, they encounter the confrontation between the poet's thirst for freedom and accuracy in perception and the prosaic society's insistence on rhetoric and routine. In the densely patterned advanced countries of the modern world, the dominant posture toward experience is (and perhaps must be) a manipulative one. The worlds of man and of nature are alike to be reined and exploited in the service of abstract goals such as "progress" or "profit" or national might. Countering this posture is the poet's sense of wonder and delight, his being in the world to enjoy and understand rather than to achieve. Yurii spoke earlier of his despair at those who would "reshape life"; similarly, Hans Speier articulates the poet's core attitude: "Who is the poet? We are hardly prepared to learn or inclined to believe that the poet is the forgotten You and I who know of nature before it is tortured. In the poet we crucify that part of ourselves which reminds us of knowledge we have forfeited, that knowledge of nature which does *not* enable us to change the world around us, but to understand it and live in it."[9]

Pasternak expresses the poetic perception and its inherent antagonism toward the programming of life in a variety of ways. Here, for instance, he shows us Lara's vivid appreciation of the earth in her role as poet, lover of a poet, possibly mother of a poet: "For a moment she rediscovered the purpose of her life. She was here on earth to grasp the meaning of its wild enchantment and to call each thing by its right name, or, if this were not within her power, to give birth out of love for life to successors who would do it in her place."[10] "To call each thing by its right name" is perhaps the noblest and most complex result of an essential simplicity. The poet as namer is the poet in his most tangible guise. Threaded through *Doctor Zhivago* is the recurrent theme of simplicity, naturalness, individuality, the taste for the concrete; always these are posed as the desirable alternatives to the antipoetic ideology of inflated rhetoric and massive unconcern for the small, merely human things that actually comprise the fabric of experience. Thus we hear Zhivago's impatience with abstractions, and in it an echo of the Hemingway fatigued by the rhetoric of patriotism; Zhivago is oppressed by "the meaningless dullness of human eloquence." Or, again, the artist expresses his appetite for existential immediacy, reminiscent of both Hemingway and Camus: "Man is born to live, not to prepare for life." And in his most explicit rendering of this theme, he asks,

> What is it that prevents me from being a doctor and a writer? I think it is not our privations or our wanderings or our unsettled lives, but the prevalent spirit of high-flown rhetoric, which has spread everywhere—

phrases such as "the dawn of the future," "the building of a new world," "the torch-bearers of mankind." The first time you hear such talk you think "What breadth of imagination, what richness!" But in fact it's so pompous just because it is so unimaginative and second-rate.

Only the familiar transformed by genius is truly great. . . . In 'Onegin's Travels' we read:

Now my ideal is the housewife,
My greatest wish, a quiet life
And a big bowl of cabbage soup.

What I have come to like best in the whole of Russian literature is the childlike Russian quality of Pushkin and Chekhov, the modest reticence in such high sounding matters as the ultimate purpose of mankind or their own salvation. It isn't that they didn't think about these things, and to good effect, but to talk about such things seemed to them pretentious, presumptuous. Gogol, Tolstoy, Dostoievsky looked restlessly for the meaning of life, and prepared for death and drew conclusions. Pushkin and Chekhov, right up to the end of their lives, were absorbed in the current, specific tasks imposed on them by their vocation as writers, and in the course of fulfilling these tasks they lived their lives, quietly, treating both their lives and their work as private, individual matters, of no concern to anyone else. And these individual things have since become of concern to all, and their works, like apples picked while they are green, have ripened of themselves, mellowing gradually and growing richer in meaning.[11]

In Pasternak's religious vision he reiterates the poet's cherished treason toward the idea of the state as supreme reality: "In that new way of living and new form of society, which is born of the heart, and which is called the Kingdom of Heaven, there are no nations, there are only individuals."[12] It is probably true that for the poet today whether Christian or pagan, there are no nations. Fidelity to the individual as the highest good, with all this implies about the importance of private experience, makes the artist by definition a suspicious and marginal citizen. His central allegiances simply lie elsewhere. And the nature of the poet's craft is such that he cannot dissemble; in his role as writer he must tell the truth or effectively cease to exist. He must willingly abandon himself to the apprehension of things as they are; his obdurate innocence and openness closely parallel the qualities demanded in the highest of human activities, the one so near to artistic creativity, the act of loving. As Robert Frost said about the writing of a poem, "The figure is the same as for love."

Love as Duty and Treason

Doctor Zhivago is ultimately a love story, and the relation of Yurii to Lara embodies and underscores all the novel's other themes. Lara-Antipova is surely one of the compelling figures of recent world literature. The mystery of Lara seems essential to her heroism, her almost mythic quality: here is a woman about whom we know everything and nothing. Lara's life history is most explicit, yet her personality is somehow shadowed, evanescent. We apprehend her in her effect on Zhivago, rather than in direct confrontation with the reader; her words and acts are in a sense less real to us than is Zhivago's image of her. In this vein, and bizarre as the comparison might at first appear, Lara is reminiscent of that other real-unreal protagonist of the modern novel, that son of God so true to his conception of himself and so false to others' conception of him, Jay Gatsby. And like Gatsby, Lara, who wants always to be life-size, a natural creature, emerges as larger than life. To her accrue the dreams of men, as well as their just observations. She is at once the tangibly desired and the intangibly desirable.

If the first meaning of Lara is mystery, as the focus of Zhivago's transcendental impulses, the second is simplicity. Not, to be sure, the simplicity of unawareness: hers is rather the simplicity of directness, concretion, fundamental disregard of the self. For Lara is a natural thing, a creature who wants to know the world as it is and to speak of it as it is. Svetlana Alliluyeva expresses Lara's abiding naturalness: "Lara, Lara, you were life and love, you were a swift-flowing river, you were a woodland full of the golden sun, and a rowan tree of fiery red—how you warmed everyone around you, how good people felt when you were near. But no one could protect you, nor could you protect yourself."[13]

Almost always, the primary quality that attracts Zhivago to her is her self-containedness, her beautiful control of life as a graceful dance of self-surrender. So it was in the library at Varykino, when the fated lovers rehearsed a first physical union that was at the same time a psychological reunion.

Yurii Andreievich noticed again what he had observed long ago in Meliuzeievo, "She does not want to please or look beautiful," he thought. "She despises all that aspect of a woman's nature; it's as though she were punishing herself for being lovely. But this proud hostility to herself makes her ten times more irresistible. . . . How well she does everything! She reads not as if reading were the highest human activity, but as if it were the simplest possible thing, a thing that even animals could do. As if she were carrying water from a well, or peeling potatoes."[14]

If Lara is mysterious, simple, natural, she is above all *real*. Her recurrent thrust into Zhivago's history embodies the tangible quality of the real and private, as opposed to the windy public rhetoric of revolutionary slogans. Perhaps all reality is essentially a private reality, or perhaps private and public reality are simply distinct things. In any event, Lara's realness seems to go together with her fierce privacy; she is for Zhivago a sanctuary, a refreshing and direct refuge from the importunities of bourgeois hollowness and Bolshevik fervor alike. It is Lara whose sex and sensibility make up to Zhivago for life with Tonia and her family, for what Frances Cornford called in another connection "the long littleness of life." And it is Lara whose "isness" rescues the hero from ideology and confirms his priorities of value.

Yurii and Lara, like Camus's rebel, reject the claims of abstract ideological principles and grandiose schemes for explaining or altering collective history. Indeed, *Doctor Zhivago's* root theme may be conceived as a series of tensions between a supposed public good and a felt private good, between a public duty to alter men's destinies and a private duty to enact one's own destiny. Thus we see in the lovers a repeated phrasing of the basic conflict: the poet versus the state; the concrete versus the abstract; the modest versus the grandiose; the private love versus the public duty. Indeed, Zhivago's (and Pasternak's) actual "crime" against the Soviet state is not opposition to the common weal, or even to official dogma, but rather a defiant withdrawal into private experience. This withdrawal into a precious interpersonal universe—the universe bounded by making love, writing a poem, reflecting upon natural things—is more truly subversive of the established order than any counterrevolutionary manifesto. Like the lovers of George Orwell's *1984*, Yurii and Lara assert the most dangerous of all counterclaims in an age of ideology and overarching statehood—the claim of a "merely personal" love. To betray the state or promote an alternative ruling order are orthodox heresies; with these the state can understand and cope. But withdrawal into the immediacy of private need and primary communion with some few others strikes at the very premises of a highly organized society.

The meaning of Lara is the antithesis of the collective claims upon Zhivago and of the conventional furniture of mundane social life. She is what every poet needs and few find—a conspiratorial companion in full rebellion against political dogma and comfortable middle-class morality. With Lara, and only with her, Yurii comes wholly alive, alert, conscious of his talent as physician and artist. Their zest together, their inward flight to sensual and intellectual reality, is underlined by the description of the true foe. Strelnikov, the rigid revolutionary, embodies all that is unnatural and hateful:

And if he were really to do good, he would have needed, in addition to his principles, a heart capable of violating them—a heart which knows only of particular, not of general cases, and which achieves greatness in little actions. . . . Filled with the loftiest aspirations from his childhood, he had looked upon the world as a vast arena where everyone competed for perfection, keeping scrupulously to the rules. When he found that this was not so, it did not occur to him that his conception of the world order might have been oversimplified. He nursed his grievance and with it the ambition to judge between life and the dark forces that distorted it, and to be life's champion and avenger. . . . Embittered by his disappointment, he was armed by the revolution.[15]

Lara's meaning is to be tender. Hers and Yurii's is the gentlest love. They move together in grave inclination, in the ancient rehearsal Archibald MacLeish evokes in his "Ars Poetica":

For love
The leaning grasses and two lights above the sea

Her meaning is also to endure, to meet experience with the simplicity and ardor of Yurii's poem *Hamlet*: "To live life to the end is not a childish task."[16] In their loving duty Yurii and Lara remain faithful to one another. As poetic spirits they sustain, too, a love for life itself—a delicious and terrifying melting into the green and snowy cathedral of the natural world.

8

Albert Camus

Personality as Creative Struggle

> The struggle itself toward the heights is enough to fill a man's
> heart. One must imagine Sisyphus happy.
>
> Camus, *The Myth of Sisyphus*

For Camus, as *The Myth of Sisyphus* makes explicit, man is
alive only in his struggle, only in his defiant engagement with a
world he never made but in which he must live. In pursuit of self-
awareness and competence—not mastery—vis-à-vis his environment, man is not pursuing happiness but already enjoying
all of that blessed condition he will ever know. For Camus
happiness is recognized in activity, not achieved as a state of
being; personality is renewed in process, not honed to a finished
symmetry.

Starting from scratch, Camus asks how a man can and
should live, how he can regard himself, what stance he can take
toward the physical universe, how he can work, how he can be
related to other persons. Camus questions the very possibility
and worth of living, and he does this in radically naked, direct
fashion. Although he is by no means a formal existentialist philosopher, he adopts the attitude of deliberately naïve inquiry into
the nature of reality. What is the design of the world as directly
experienced? Is human life desirable, and if so how may it be
conducted?

The Philosophical Context

He begins without assumptions to guarantee the worth and meaning of personality. Camus perceives the universe as chaotic, without pattern and without any significance other than its meaning to the individual as experienced day by day. He casts off the solace of religious doctrine, of political salvationism, of a belief in an evolutionary progress in men's affairs or any man's internal development. He insists on a life without illusion, a life of strict honesty toward the self and stoic perseverance toward a witless universe.

In this life, personality is both ground and product of a harsh battle, a unique integrity to be created, renewed, rewon in a quotidian fight. The solitary man is involved in a struggle without cease, a perilous war of attrition against meaninglessness, brutality, injustice, and ultimate loss of nerve. Camus exhorts us to stop the sacrifice of human beings on the altars of ideology, to live for ourselves and others and not for abstract dictates. Thus he sees personality as neither a "given" nor a "bought," but as an ongoing achievement. Because the odds against achieving them are so long, right conduct and inner grace are precious trophies to be burnished and constantly retrieved from the flux of existence.

Camus cannot be understood without placing him in the context of modern European man. He is able to ask such searching questions and grapple so vigorously with social psychological problems only because he grew to manhood in a social order stripped of illusion. The stripping involved not only the renunciation of ancient religious and philosophical verities. It also involved the intrusion of total warfare, totalitarian politics, all the wretched spasms of man's inhumanity to man. Essentially, Camus finds that old answers have failed, old myths have become less satisfying. Neither the religion of Christianity nor the ideology of Communism, he maintains, affords contemporary man a satisfactory framework for explaining life or a reliable guide for conduct toward his fellows.

Camus's days spanned the interwar hope in political utopianism, and the crushing of that hope in the torments of the thirties and the Second World War with its sequels of rehabilitation and destruction. In effect, Camus says, we have been deceived. The universe is not intelligible on the basis of divine plan, and human relations are not intelligible on the basis of historical drift or ideological commandment. The issue is not picking up the pieces but inventing new pieces better tailored to living beings. Camus does not despair, even when his superb intelligence gives him many reasons for despairing. Instead he faces the world; he looks within himself. He dares the most extreme questions and does not flinch from blunt answers. Above all, he continues being a man; he survives with ironic fortitude.

The grandeur and excitement of Camus's conception of personality are rooted in his view of life as tentative and precarious. To him personality has added savor because it is so palpably life in the presence of death, existence with the omnipresent alternative of suicide. An individual, realizing that life is absurd, can get out of it; he can destroy himself, resign from the game, and end forever the struggle to understand, to create a self and a meaning. Camus argues that the question of suicide is the first philosophical problem. It is the first psychological one as well. If that option is chosen, then obviously no other problems need be resolved. The fully aware man in a meaningless universe has in some sense this first great freedom to choose. His life is lived in the shadow of the choice; if he is determined to go on, one might say that he has affirmed the idea of personality and won the kernel of individual process.

Camus recommends rebellion as the proper philosophical stance toward life. The act of suicide is to him an illegitimate way out of the human predicament. Rather than voluntarily retiring from what seems to be an absurd situation—rational man opposed to irrational universe—the individual should rebel at lack of meaning. This rebellion is not only, or even chiefly, a defiance of political axiom or conventional authority. It is really a rebellion against indignity, against the impotent and irrational and unmanly. Camus holds counteraction to be the wise and courageous reply by the individual to all the senseless terrors of this world. Not being given a finished personality, a revealed reason for living, or an inevitable design in nature, man must create for himself his own vital rationale. His building and maintenance of a viable personality is the nobler because he recognizes the brevity of life. In the inner conviction that his days are short, his triumphs impermanent, his predicament absurd, he yet defies his condition. If he is fully aware and spiritually creative, he wins the short-run battle to be human even as he necessarily loses the long-run battle to be fixedly right, to be in any sense immortal.

Strangers and Plagues

The imaginative achievement of Camus's too short career is embodied in a series of novels, plays, and essays. His version of personality and social conduct may be traced most clearly in two superb novels, *The Stranger* and *The Plague*, and two central essays, *The Myth of Sisyphus* and *The Rebel*. These writings are in the very first rank of modern European literature and made their author a Nobel Laureate while he was still in his early forties. They afford us the testimony of a gifted artist on the situation we are in: What is the problem for personality, for the person-in-action? They give us also Camus's implicit conclusions about what we are to do: In the problematic circumstance of modern life, how can and should a fit individual behave? It might be said that Camus enunciates a rather special psychology, the psychology of the artist or intellectual. Yet not only does he stress the continuity between the artist and everyman, but as we see repeatedly in history, the problems of the artist at a given time are likely to be the endemic problems of a slightly later era.

The Stranger is the short novel that first brought Camus to wide attention. It is a compact, poetic, merciless account of the absurd man in his first realization of absurdity. The hero, Meursault, has discovered the open secret that the universe is without meaning. His nihilistic response is to abolish value from his personal life, to live a hedonistic but passionless calculus. In personality Meursault is passive, a detached observer of life who satisfies his biological needs in a joyless shadow play. Ennui and fatigue, coupled with a sardonic half-interest in the motives of those around him, are his abiding characteristics. Under a hot, relentless Algerian sun, in a universe as drained of vitality as it is drained of meaning, Meursault enacts a senseless career. There is no reason for him to act as he does; but in his own terms there is equally no reason for him to act otherwise.

In Camus's stranger, we find the individual who is estranged from the universe—not one who merely dislikes his part in the scheme of things but one who denies that the schemes of nature or society or his role in them have any significance whatever.

In plot, *The Stranger* recounts a simple, stark chain of un-witting doom. Meursault is first encountered as he reacts to his mother's death, and our first clue to his nature is exactly this: he does *not* react. He knows what he is expected to feel and to do, but he goes through the motions of mourning in a numb, trancelike state, feeling no emotion stronger than annoyance. His mother's death is an imposition upon him, for he must trouble himself to appear grieved, to accept condolence, to pretend that the end of her life and their relationship is a mean-ingful event. Throughout the vigil and the funeral, Meursault preserves a flat level of affect. His emotional neurasthenia is seen as he apologizes to his superior for taking time off from work to go to the funeral, as he refuses to look at his mother's body, as he plods sweating to the church. The tone is manifest in his ex-change with the undertaker (Meursault is the narrator):

"Sun's pretty bad today, ain't it?"
"Yes," I said.
After a while he asked: "Is it your mother we're burying?"
"Yes," I said again.
"What was her age?"
"Well, she was getting on." As a matter of fact, I didn't know exactly how old she was.[1]

Meursault proceeds to have a desultory love affair, beginning immediately after his mother's burial. Toward the girl, Marie, he again feels nothing; he sees her claim upon him as an invasion, a violation of his desire not to be engaged with the world.

When he is offered a better job, he refuses. His job means nothing more than onerous routine, an interference with sleep and again an invasion of his passive privacy. Indeed, the idea of "better" or "worse" among his activities and relationships is quite foreign to him. Any thing is as good as any other thing.

Without reason, he is drawn into visiting the seaside with a casual friend, who fears a violent encounter with some Arabs. He arms himself against a possible clash. Strolling the beach, he comes upon one of the Arabs. He thinks he sees the glint of a knife, and in the dizzying heat he fires and kills. Brought to trial, he offers no defense. He has seemingly murdered without motive, but his conviction and sentence to death hinge less on the act itself than on his obdurate lack of remorse. Meursault is in fact convicted for not *caring*; his guilt is in his detachment from life: "Replying to questions, he said that I'd declined to see Mother's body, I'd smoked cigarettes and slept, and drunk *café au lait*. It was then I felt a sort of wave of indignation spreading through the courtroom, and for the first time I understood that I was guilty."[2] At his trial, the most damning indictment against him is his disregard of social convention; his unfeeling behavior at his mother's funeral is emphasized by the prosecutor to show his essential inhumanity. Only as his execution is imminent does he begin to feel the attractions of life. Life in the presence of death takes on color, pleasure, a sense of purpose in his resolution to die well and justly.

Meursault is a nihilist, holding the philosophy of the ultimately estranged individual. He represents what Camus elsewhere distinguishes as two of the logical implications of nihilism: *rational egoism*, a strategic and utter selfishness oriented solely to the convenience and comfort of the self; and *annihilation*, the destruction of the existing order. All that happens in *The Stranger* is viewed entirely in its implications for Meursault, who is really unable to participate in anything that occurs outside his own musings, his internal dialogue. So self-entrapped is he that he is constantly fatigued, longing for the rest and sleep that shut out the boring, repellent world and excuse him to be alone with himself.

If Meursault is the rational egoist, he is also the agent of annihilation. His final assertion of the lack of meaning in his life is to commit a meaningless murder. Murder is the ultimate act of destruction, first of another personality and then, by inexorable implication, of the self. To Camus, murder is, like suicide, an illegitimate path of rebellion against existence. In *The Rebel* he describes it thus: "It is the limit that can be reached but once, after which one must die. The rebel has only one way of reconciling himself with his act of murder if he allows himself to be led into performing it: to accept his own death and sacrifice."[3]

This is precisely what Meursault does. And it is senseless: the victim is a stranger to the killer, just as the killer is a stranger to the universe. Murder is the culmination of a search for total freedom of action. It is the limiting case of nihilism, expressed by the radical statement: "Awareness of the absurd, when we first claim to deduce a rule of behavior from it, makes murder seem a matter of indifference, to say the least, and hence possible."[4] If all men are mortal and if life has no meaning, what natural design or moral law has a murderer in fact contravened? As Meursault muses before killing the Arab: "And just then it crossed my mind that one might fire, or not fire—and it would come to absolutely the same thing."[5]

Meursault might be seen as a skeletal personality, an individual purged of convention and delusion. He has a certain uncluttered purity, has faced existence and cast off the trappings of older images of man. But his pristine self is without positive force; he represents the first stage of absurdity, an awareness of the plight. His single initiating act is mistaken: he has used the freedom afforded by absurd cognition in an illicit way. Meursault reconciles himself with the murderous act by "accepting his own death and sacrifice." In this acceptance he begins for the first time to feel, to have active likes and dislikes. His approaching death brings him a feeling of certainty. Somehow cleansed by his willful act and its fated consequence, he opens his heart to the "benign indifference of the universe." Meursault gains awareness of his existential freedom to choose at the moment when he is about to lose it. Paradoxically in a logical sense but understandably from a psychodynamic viewpoint, he enjoys subjective freedom in the only well-defined social role he has ever known—the role of the prisoner awaiting the guillotine. Gone are the ambiguities, the tensions of unresolved desire, the anxieties of choice.

The Stranger may represent a clearing away of deadwood, a farewell to divinely assured man and historically complacent man. Perhaps such a destructive leave-taking is necessary to blot out traditional models of personality and traditional bondage to blind social forms. Meursault sees clearly although he acts wrongly. But Camus does not stop with this fearsome surgery, this devilishly bold attempt to return to the primitive issues of man's

existence. *The Stranger* states the case for the individual's freedom to make himself and to find refreshment in a naïve, poetic
experience of the universe—as if nature and society were truly
confronted for the first time, with all patterns to be questioned,
all actions to be newly evaluated. But Meursault's response is a
monstrous error. Camus's next novel, and probably his finest,
The Plague, is in an important sense an answer to the dilemma
posed by *The Stranger*: How can the individual find meaning in
an indifferent cosmos, and how can he conceive his life in terms
that make life preferable to death?

Meursault has simple, sensuous joys and direct perceptivity.
The heroes of *The Plague* add to these rudimentary virtues a
higher pair—the sense of vocation and the capacity for love.
Their situation demands the exercise of devoted intelligence and
energy, for it involves not merely the problems of living a normal
life but also the high challenge of pestilence—the active forces
of death. In plot, *The Plague* is as bare and simple as *The
Stranger*: an epidemic of bubonic plague is visited upon the city
of Oran, and the narrative tells us how various citizens behave in
a situation of extreme threat. Camus makes it clear, however, that
plague as physical disease symbolizes all the inhumanities and
deaths to which men are recurrently exposed; the human condition is vulnerable to war, cruelty, injustice, lack of love, lack of
purpose, and all these are summed up in the plague bacillus.
Many persons are followed through the long months of epidemic
terror with its isolation, fear, and suffering unto death. And the
city itself is followed, the human community under stress in its
shifting moods and colors. We are told, basically, how people
respond to ultimate threat: how they live with it, fight it, die from
it.

Camus traces the climactic period in the lives of lovers,
criminals, priests, the young and the aged, observers, officials,
and healers. Oran is walled off from the outside world, turned in
upon itself to cope with a pestilence that at its peak carries off
hundreds of victims each day. The first and last torments of the
victims are described in brutal clinical detail, always in the
context of personal history and tangible urban environment. In
essence, *The Plague* is a grim morality tale, understated and told
without pomposity or sentimentality; it is, strikingly, a morality

tale in which morals are constantly offered up for testing and reevaluation, in which codes are questioned under the last duress of imminent death. Above all, it is the story of a fight, of the strategies people adopt to combat a fierce disease that threatens each of them in its capricious path through the population of Oran.

A model of personality and a model of conduct are implicit in the leading characters of The Plague. The host of individuals all reveal facets of Camus's conception, but the core is most firmly embodied in two men—the physician, Dr. Rieux, who is the novel's chief figure and purported narrator, and the rather mysterious Tarrou, a person of no fixed occupation and therefore a poet or saint. Rieux and Tarrou are distinguished by a quiet heroism, an unobtrusive courage that gains an added force from contrast with the lurid ravages of the plague itself. The novel recounts the impact of disease on Oran, the disjunctions in private lives and community organization, and especially the strenuous exertions of Rieux and Tarrou in the care of the afflicted. It is overtly a losing battle: the epidemic runs a long and virulent course, and the healers cannot save those they love best or even one another. But they never surrender to the plague, never cease to be rebels against death. It is just this endless rebellion in the service of life that constitutes the moral imperative for Camus: to live without appeal to absolutes of faith or reason; to see as clearly as possible; to avoid giving others pain; to fight plague wherever it appears.

The idea of personality as a process and of happiness as a by-product of struggle is integral to both The Plague and the brief philosophical essay The Myth of Sisyphus. In a sense, Sisyphus's task—endlessly rolling a rock to the top of a mountain, whence it would fall back down of its own weight—is a mythic analogue of Rieux's vocation of healing. Dr. Rieux, too, realizes that all must be done again, that the epidemic will carry off many of those he has treated and that other epidemics will occur. Yet he sees the fight against all our plagues as both necessary and intrinsically rewarding. He and Tarrou inherit Camus's notion of "humiliated thought"; they do not believe themselves utterly right, are not arrogant or all-knowing. They humbly recognize that they may not always even identify the plague correctly, but

Tarrou states their duty: "On this earth there are pestilences and there are victims, and it's up to us, so far as possible, not to join forces with the pestilences."[6]

Fulfillment for these heroes lies in struggle. One must imagine them to be, like Sisyphus, happy. Their happiness, like his, rests on two primary supports that enable them to endure in a world without ultimate meaning or hope of ultimate achievement. Sisyphus, says Camus, glories in his freedom from illusion, in the concrete shape of his natural world, in the tangible reality of his chore. And so it is with Rieux and Tarrou: their morale is refreshed by acute awareness and by obviously important work. Both their consciousness and their labor are manifestations of love, although in modesty and toughness they do not speak of love. Rieux, the healer, speaks of his goals: "Salvation's much too big a word for me. I don't aim so high. I'm concerned with man's health; and for me his health comes first."[7]

Tarrou, the poet who has joined in the grinding labor against the plague, speaks of his morality. It is the morality of the artist, the true perceiver, informed by love of victims and hatred of oppressors. "Consciousness," by which he means the maximum of alertness, sensitivity, and knowledge, is seen as a goal for personality.

The soul of the murderer is blind; and there can be no true goodness nor true love without the utmost clear sightedness. . . . And I know, too, that we must keep endless watch on ourselves lest in a careless moment we breathe in somebody's face and fasten the infection on him. What's natural is the microbe. All the rest—health, integrity, purity (if you like)—is a product of the human will, of a vigilance that must never falter. The good man, the man who infects hardly anyone, is the man who has the fewest lapses of attention.[8]

And when Rieux, wondering at the poet's involvement in public health when he appears to be a man without faith or announced altruism, demands, "Your code of morals? What code?" Tarrou replies, "Comprehension."[9]

The Social Psychology of Extremity

Camus's fiction portrays extreme situations; his men are always living in high tension—"at the stretch," as Rieux describes the sensations of an attentive plague fighter. In this vein, his imaginative work corresponds to the harsh angularity of his essays, the pushing of limits that marks the confrontation of the absurd in root philosophical terms. Distortion of reality, grotesque happenstance, the polarity of evil and holiness, a social stage denuded of the petty comforts of conventional life—all these are characteristic of modern literature in its attempt to persuade men of the enormity of their condition. It is as if the felt confusion of values, the revelation of evil in war and totalitarianism, the sense of being somehow lost in a disorganized social universe were translated into imaginative chaos and bitter unrealism.

One might suppose that in showing us a deranged world the artist is akin to the clinical psychologist, illuminating normal functioning by seizing on the accentuated lessons—and lesions—of the abnormal. Erikson has justified our concern with the atypical by recalling Freud's image of the broken crystal, which reveals its structure best in a shattered state. We have evidence too, from studies of behavior in natural disasters such as fires and tornadoes, that the actions of men under profound stress are relevant to theories of behavior in the large.

There are at least three levels on which Camus's presentation of human extremity may be discussed: as a veridical rendering, exaggerated only in superficial detail, of certain timeless problems inherent in the human condition; as a reflection of issues that are specific to twentieth-century urban man, issues sharpened for us by the sacrifice of moderation and familiar habitude in fictional guise; and as a study of de facto extremity, of the way people act in situations that are avowedly abnormal and catastrophic.

The first of these alternatives would perhaps be most appropriate to Camus's explicit intent, although obviously these ways of seeing are not mutually exclusive. His protagonists are in the kinds of situations men have always been in; they differ from the classical heroes of tragic circumstance only in their extraordinary awareness of their plight, which is bound up with their terrifying freedom from dogma. They are in the plight of Oedipus, but there is no pattern of justice and injustice. They are in the plight of Job, but there is no God, however deaf. They are in the plight of Lear, but there is no accepted measure of nobility in character or of value in the affairs of men. All of Camus's heroes rehearse the eternal ordeals that are inseparable from being human. Meursault, the stranger, poses the question of intelligibility in the universe: Where is the design that makes one act preferable to another? Is life to be chosen over death? Rieux, the plague doctor, announces again the problem of Job: Why should there be senseless suffering, why the death of a child from bubonic plague? In *The Plague*, too, we are asked the basic moral question: What do men owe to life and to one another? Underlying such traditionally formulated issues and implicit in much of Camus's work is the fundamental dualism of the human being as at once animal and angel—the dislocation between virtuosity in symbolic behavior and bondage to physiological imperatives, especially as expressed in man's persistent estrangement from the immediacies of experience. The Camus hero's task is well expressed in the ancient observation of Heraclitus: "Man is estranged from that with which he is most familiar and he must continuously seek to rediscover it." The rediscovery of the familiar in the light of cosmic indifference and the primitive seeking of a way to live may be seen as the chief assignments of the absurd man.

Contemporary dilemmas, the second possible ordering of Camus's fictional themes, center on a truism of modern literary criticism: men exist among a confusion of values, a confusion so pronounced that some live *without* values. The novelist covertly and the critic overtly deplore the lack of a consensus of values in the modern world. To it they refer the anxious questioning of the self-conscious hero and the difficulty of artistic communication in a society bereft of symbolic communion. Since men no longer share a religious world view or any other consistent, received hierarchy of values, they cannot agree on the meaning of symbols or share a recognized set of terms for the interpretation of experience. The widespread apprehension of "normlessness" roughly indicated by the sociological concept of *anomie* is at the heart of the absurd man's being; he questions all things, including the legitimacy of the questions themselves. Again, we have for exemplars Meursault in *The Stranger* and Camus in his essays.

The arrangement of social organization that is often called "mass society" is the setting for the absurd hero's interrogation of the life around him. This social web, now seemingly so dense it stifles, now so thin it leaves the individual gasping for sustenance, is seen as both cause and effect of the breakdown of values. Its trite features include the depersonalization that characterizes large numbers of people engaged in relationships of fragmented, transitory cast; in sociological terms, this is a society marked by many "secondary relationships," interpersonal contacts that emphasize a particular aspect or role of the individual— buyer and seller, for instance—at the expense of his unique personality. This taking of parts for wholes is often related to what Stein called "the eclipse of community," the feeling that we are not now members of one another in anything like the fashion of smaller, intimate, face-to-face groupings. No one in *The Stranger*, including his mother, is at all close to Meursault; he soon discovers that people have nothing to say to one another.

There are other facets of life today that help create the sense of extremity and the burden of loneliness. We are at once overstimulated and stultified: overstimulated by the plethora of inputs from the mass media of communication, we are unable to find a quiet place; stultified by the routine requirements of work in large bureaucracies, we are unable to exert creative will. Over all these features hovers the shadow of rapid change, as life slips through and around the person, as society changes the rules before the player has mastered the game.

Of final, special relevance today is the set of issues Erikson terms "the problem of ego-identity." The questions of knowing who one is and why gnaw the hero in fiction as in life. All of Camus's characters search for self-knowledge, regarding their identities as fleeting and their postures in the eyes of others as problematic. Individuals are unsure of "placing" themselves and others in a fluid social environment. One's work may carry a label but not a seal of worthful conviction. Personal identity, personality itself, is a struggle without end.

Finally, we may see Camus's landscape as a realistic disaster area. In this perspective the novels are instructive commentaries on social disarticulation. Disaster in *The Stranger* is personal— not mass murder and guilt but the death of one Arab and the

prospective demise of his killer. Yet the shock of disaster, the
changed orientation of Meursault as temporary survivor, the
coping behavior of the persons involved are illustrative of general human processes in extreme situations. *The Plague* is much
more nearly an analogue of social disaster on a wide scale and
is, indeed, almost a text for community life under duress. Here
we find the slow reluctance to recognize disaster as the pestilence is assimilated to normal events for as long as possible. We
find the shock of definition—the plague comes to be called a
plague—and the numbed acceptance of mass fatalities. There is
heroism and competent adaptation; there is also cowardice,
apathy, and random frenzy. Most importantly, *The Plague* reveals
the way communities pull themselves together constructively
under disaster and the way individuals act with a competence
and generous efficiency. Here the novelist foretells many of the
generalizations that have been more recently derived from scientific field studies of disaster. Camus teaches what research affirms: the stress of abnormal events calls forth assured coping
more often than panic; the challenge of extremity may stimulate
both a firmer communal bondage and a more ample individual
capacity to deal with the environment.

The final paragraphs of *The Plague* give point to the idea
that extreme situations reveal much that is positive in human
character. What Camus says here is pertinent to classical and
contemporary philosophical extremity as well as to overt disaster; it also leads us toward his conception of personality as
unresting struggle. The citizens of Oran are celebrating the lifting
of the plague.

And it was in the midst of shouts rolling against the terrace wall in
massive waves that waxed in volume and duration, while cataracts of
colored fire fell thicker through the darkness, that Dr. Rieux resolved to
compile this chronicle, so that he should not be one of those who hold
their peace but should bear witness in favor of those plague-stricken
people; so that some memorial of the injustice and outrage done them
might endure; and to state quite simply what we learn in a time of
pestilence: that there are more things to admire in men than to despise.
. . . None the less, he knew that the tale he had to tell could not be one
of a final victory. It could be only the record of what had had to be done,
and what assuredly would have to be done again in the neverending
fight against terror and its relentless onslaughts, despite their personal

afflictions, by all who, while unable to be saints but refusing to bow down to pestilences, strive their utmost to be healers.[10]

It is clear that Camus as poet enunciates neither a formula for personality nor a detailed model for conduct. His laws of human behavior are the common law of precedent, of hard-gained experience, not the code law of civil postulate. Yet the student of personality and society discovers in his creations both a valid statement of existential boundaries and a wise, fresh proposal for action.

Life is involvement. Personality is the process of being actively engaged with one's world. What Camus asks is that the individual exercise conscious choice and that he persist in the exercise despite his recognition of man's frailty and his knowledge that there are no ultimate certainties toward which he may steer. Sisyphus and Dr. Rieux are alike in their endurance, their acceptance of a work to be done all again, and their glorying in the struggle for its own sake. In Allport's words, their motives are "functionally autonomous," not resting on instinctual drive or the promise of distant applause but on intrinsic satisfactions.

The themes of engagement and effortful choice are complemented by a stoic humanism that enjoins healing. Dr. Rieux is a symbol of this defiant refusal to neglect the daily needs of others. An admirable personality is a committed one, spending itself in the grim battle against plagues of all kinds. Camus holds, essentially, that the individual fulfills himself in loving devotion to other men; but this devotion is not an abstract, bloodless love geared to religious dicta or vague humanitarian sentiments. Rather, it is the watchful care and energetic construction of the man who lives every day fully, sees every choice in its charged human significance. As Camus writes in The Rebel: "This insane generosity is the generosity of rebellion, which unhesitatingly gives the strength of its love and without a moment's delay refuses injustice. Its merit lies in making no calculation, distributing everything it possesses to life and to living men. It is thus that it is prodigal in its gifts to men to come. Real generosity toward the future lies in giving all to the present."[11]

The capstone of this orientation to personality and conduct is the idea of creativity. Camus takes the artist as prototype of the free man who glories in the struggle to be alive and to clarify reality. He says the human will has "no other purpose than to maintain awareness." For him this is precisely what personality means—the fully alert man engaged in war against disorder, sloth, blindness. And this personality truly makes itself in an endless nervous process; it must do so, since it has no external props, no absolutes, no secure resting place. Awareness implies a heady freedom. Just because the modern individual is in a hard world and has foregone the soothing illusions of the past, he is free to choose. He can be self-generating, can be an exemplar of the "pro-action" that Henry Murray opposes to the traditional psychological model of reactive man. Thus Camus explains the creative man:

Of all the schools of patience and lucidity, creation is the most effective. It is also the staggering evidence of man's sole dignity: the dogged revolt against his condition, perseverance in an effort considered sterile. It calls for a daily effort, self-mastery, a precise estimate of the limits of truth, measure, and strength. It constitutes an *ascesis*. All that "for nothing," in order to repeat and mark time. But perhaps the great work of art has less importance in itself than in the ordeal it demands of a man and the opportunity it provides him of overcoming his phantoms and approaching a little closer to his naked reality.[12]

Camus's psychology is not susceptible to easy summary. It is a protean conception of man, shrewdly cognizant of all the deficits in the human condition and still aware of the surpluses. It emphasizes the individual's capacity to act on his environment and to order himself toward substantial achievement. Camus exalts the creative act, seeing it as the healthy essence of being human. He has plumbed the black recesses of personality and known the shock of horror at man's inhumanity, yet held to a sturdy secular faith in the individual will. The unfinished business of every man, personality is growth and constant learning; Camus states, "The only original rule of life today: to learn to live and to die, and, in order to be a man, to refuse to be a god."[13] Exhibiting the true humility of the audacious questioner, Camus stresses growth and openness to experience. And he comes at the end to a profound optimism, grounded not in feckless hope but in the deep endurance of sentient personality.

9

Samuel Beckett

The Social Psychology of Emptiness

"Bleak" is the word for Beckett, you say? "Yes," one can only reply, as far as the manifest content of his drama is concerned. But great antipathies do often betray intense affinities: no one could hate man so much if he were not sometime suffused with love for him. Think of those who have savaged man, those whose corrosive violence has threatened to reduce him entirely; think of Dean Swift, of Voltaire, and of Bernard Shaw. Did they not love human beings utterly? Of course, and the measure of their love resides in their tormented railing against the gulf that divides ape from angel, the impassable and impossible distance between man as he is and man as he could be, between the frail blunderer and his infinite potential for humane grace. They are angry, indeed furious, not with man for being as he is, but for failing to be what he might be, for forfeiting his glorious possibility. And so it is with Beckett: his naked or ill-clad lumps of clay—the people of his drama—mean nothing and cannot horrify us unless they are set against a humanistic ideal of sentient man as core or effective protagonist of a patterned universe.

Perhaps the first thing that strikes us about *Waiting for Godot* or *Endgame* is the stark, barren landscape that is their stage. It is a country of "bare ruined choirs," where we are not at all sure the sweet birds sang late or soon—or ever. Stripped of all that is familiar, comforting, prosaic, it is like the gaunt plains of the moon. An alien atmosphere for alienated men. Man cannot but be estranged from this grim environment, this universe both

134

careless and hostile, whose obdurate mask is consonant with the blank wall dividing person from person and the individual from himself. How strange this terrain, how frighteningly empty of "the apple tree, the singing, and the gold." To gauge how far we have come from the warm provinces of the nineteenth century, recall only the Wessex of Thomas Hardy, where every stone and stile is laden with neighborhood memory, or the meticulously appointed drawing room of the well-made Victorian play, whose furnishings were often more real than its characters. Beckett starts with a physical setting bereft of the familiar and goes on to show us a social psychological environment equally strange and naked. As we are never sure of the geography or the chronology of the plays, because the coordinates of time and space are blurred, so we are uncertain about the ordering of human relationships. The ties of man to man are without reasonable form.

Audiences can be infuriated and upset in at least two ways—by the intrusion of what is strange and outrageous or by the omission of what is familiarly expected. The baffled outcries that greeted *Waiting for Godot* probably stemmed from both of these sources. Certainly the callousness and brutality shown one another by Beckett's players are well calculated to shock. Yet even more shocking, and disorienting like the fun-house mirrors at the amusement park, is the absence of recognizable contours in human interaction. This is a world of social and psychological deprivation, where the rations—whether of food or love, tranquillity or excitement—are perilously short. The characters live in a subsistence economy of the psyche, where the world is not so much stage as concentration camp, a concentration camp that moreover lacks both a "normal" environing society and a rationale for its misery.

The milieu of *Godot* or *Endgame* provides few orienting cues: we are left in a mysteriously empty setting, shorn of conventional social landmarks and recognizable social roles or motivations. Both plays are plotless in any orthodox sense, consisting of men who interact in a void, who have no goals except that of waiting. We are never certain for whom or for what they wait; Godot may be God or a merely secular saviour, whereas the grotesque figures of *Endgame* presumably wait only for death in a world already dead around them. A mood of suspended animation, of perpetual waiting for Godot or something nameless or sometime to come, is captured by an exchange in *Endgame*:

CLOV: Do you believe in the life to come?
HAMM: Mine was always that.[1]

The waiting bores and tires them, makes them like irritable children too long on vacation. In a desocialized society they are just barely alive. It seems that something terrible has happened to this world; it has become primitive and inhuman while retaining memory traces of a more normal existence. The unnamed threat, the unstated puzzle, remind us of science fiction in the sustained aura of danger without a face. The world as we know it has broken down, whether through war or natural catastrophe or some collective failure of nerve. So we are left with shreds of meaning, foreshortened patterns of interpersonal relations, the bare skeleton of human intercourse. Here life is rather clearly meaningless; the machine has run down. As Hamm quotes in *Endgame*, "Our revels now are ended." Yet something persists, some feeble communication and communion.

Let us look at the characteristics of this world and its people, try to see what is missing and what is left. The emptiness of the plays may by contrast help to clarify what it entails to be fully human and to live in society. Several themes are very prominent.

Deprivation

With the exception of Pozzo's bizarre feast in *Godot*, his picnic basket of wine and chicken, Beckett's people are always hungry. Listen to Hamm in *Endgame*: "I'll give you just enough to keep you from dying. You'll be hungry all the time."[2] As he says, these individuals give one another "just enough" to sustain existence. Both food and human responsiveness are in short supply; if Pozzo throws the tramps his chicken bones, so the characters throw one another the bare bones of attention and empathy. They give enough of themselves (and their resources, admittedly, are severely diminished) to keep the dialogue in limping motion and maintain a shadowy interaction, but not enough to afford any genuine satisfaction. They do not truly "reward" one another but proffer instead the thin tokens of minimal concern. There is deprivation on several levels, from the basic material needs (food, clothing), through immediate emotional needs, to, finally, complex social psychological needs for a stable human environment and a coherent world view. Carrots, turnips, bones, and hard biscuits provide the only nourishment. Clothing is odd and scanty, as in the case of Estragon's boots in *Godot*. Even simple artifacts are broken or lost, and pathetically insufficient, as Hamm's toy dog in *Endgame*. (In a sense, the distance between the mutilated toy dog and a real animal may symbolize the disparity between the stunted human interaction of the plays and a real set of social relationships.) On the emotional level, the characters consistently frustrate one another's needs for even the scantiest rewards, like the repetition of a word or a story or the running of an errand. The world of things is bare and constricted, in *Godot* a formless void, in *Endgame* a box of a room that is never clearly anchored in the landscape.

Hostility

A miasma of hostility and brutality hangs over the scene. We learn of people being beaten; they beat one another in our presence; their bodies carry old scars. Much of the conversation is hostile, upbraiding, insulting. One of the reasons it is not utterly insulting, not so entirely injurious as to rupture the fragile ties begween men, is that the characters' residue of dignity is so tiny. In Beckett's world one cannot afford the luxury of that bristling honor that makes men very sensible of insult. The people are competitive in the petty way of those living at a subsistence level or of animals battling over extremely scarce resources. They are adult forerunners of the savage boys in Golding's *Lord of the Flies*; the boys of Golding's novel become desocialized in a state of nature where they lack the restraint of adult supervision, whereas the men of Beckett's plays are desocialized because they have lost the organizing framework of a comprehensible social order. In some ways we find here a vivid image of Thomas Hobbes's hypothetical "war of each against all." Only now it is hypothesis no more, but a grim envelope of conduct.

Anarchy

This world is notable for its lack of formal organization, of political or economic patterns. Men can apparently make no appeal to the state or community, to any ordering device outside the flow of transitory interaction. Although *Godot* contains feudal overtones—Pozzo and Lucky rehearse a master-slave relationship and Godot is said to be master of an estate—one misses any reference to an organized structure of society. Even the seemingly "inevitable" social institution, the family, does not really exist: in *Endgame* Hamm's parents live in garbage cans, and they and their son could scarcely be termed a family group, although there are occasional implications of a familial past. We miss, too, the network of defined social roles on which routine relationships among individuals rest. Without roles, interaction is shapeless, tentative, tangential; people do not know what to expect from one another. Social roles embody ordered sets of anticipations. Without them or with only very rudimentary ones the individual confronts a social universe of chance. He cannot count on how others will behave, cannot gauge his actions to articulate with the actions of his opposite numbers. All that is left here, apparently, are roaming, isolated individuals or isolated pairs of men who share a bitter symbiosis. This social scene is barely recognizable in terms of the informal roles of conflict or uneasy comradery established by the faltering players.

Enervation

Energy is at a low ebb. Almost any activity is a great chore, and for several reasons: the characters are ill and crippled; they suffer from malnutrition and a pervasive fatigue; they perhaps suffer most of all from lack of motivation, from the absence of any conviction that an effort could possibly be worthwhile. There is, especially, a striking lack of vitality in the mental functions, a kind of psychological "effort syndrome" that renders thinking harmful and difficult. It is very tiring to think; one is weak and confused; a scrap of logic or a felicitous phrase represents a mighty triumph of the will.

Sexlessness

Except in vague memories of a happier time, heterosexual activity in real life or in fantasy is entirely absent. So deep is the misery of existence that sex and its consequent procreation is viewed as evil. Hamm curses his father, Nagg, for the disastrous impulse that brought him into the world: "Accursed progenitor!" and again, "Scoundrel! Why did you engender me?"[3] Beckett strongly implies in *Endgame* that Hamm, Clov, Nagg, and Nell are among the last survivors of a nuclear holocaust; the thought of bringing a child into a world that ends thus horribly is wicked and witless.

There are no female characters in either play with the exception of the pitiful mother, Nell, in *Endgame*. One has the feeling that sexual love would be beyond the capacities of these men, both because it demands more vitality than they possess and because it demands more humanity, warmth, and selflessness than they can muster. They find it hard to trust one another, to commit themselves to a love relationship or any other kind.

Yet there is an element of bawdy, the flavor of the music-hall turn or burlesque skit noted by Martin Esslin in his search for kindred vehicles in *The Theatre of the Absurd*. The bawdy is in part the complement of that pronounced undercurrent of latent and not so latent homosexuality which distinguishes an all-male society. Passages in both plays are reminiscent of other unisexual settings, notably the military, in their scatological banter and their tenderness edged with assault. Finally, one senses a distinct nostalgia, an evocation of sex once shared but now only dimly recollected. An air almost of postcoital sadness pervades the disjointed memories of what it might have been like to be human.

Hopelessness

With no future, there can be no hope. The exceptions are small, transitory "hopes" for food or the attention of other people. The longer-range hope that Godot will come is significant as the sign of hopelessness: neither players nor audience really believe he will appear, and the portents of his coming are a mad, circular dance without end. In the sequel *Endgame*, he who dares hope, even for a moment, is scorned. The plays seem to be concerned with the future; they are full of the language of waiting. But they are really about the past, a past where everything and everyone has been tried and found wanting. Hope has been proved to be without foundation. The true pathos of Beckett's stage is that everything has already happened, alternatives have been so thoroughly rehearsed that we are now at an absolute dead end, where to utter a hope is simultaneously to crush it. We are suspended in a dead center of time that offers no chronological basis for hope. Tomorrow and yesterday have a valence equal to today's—zero.

In *Waiting for Godot* the rage which greets Lucky's famous "think" stems partly from the hope implied in his words. He speaks fragments of hope—snatches of religion, reason, poetry— and even in this emasculated form they enrage the other characters, the "realists" who have renounced history and hope. The last word on hope might be Hamm's diagnosis: "Use your head, can't you, use your head, you're on earth, there's no cure for that!"[4] Beckett's world is like the dreadful prospect that made the Peruvian Indians of Vicos dance and sing dead infants to the grave in celebration of their being spared the ordeal of life.

Meaninglessness

The plays themselves are not meaningless: if they were truly so they would not have their demonstrated power to move and stimulate audiences but would be of interest solely to the clinician. Yet to the people in them the world is truly and ultimately "absurd." Nothing retains any real meaning in our ordinary use of the term, although Beckett must convey this fact in a dialogue which keeps the shadow of logic, a language possessing grammar and syntax. Although Lionel Abel, in his ingenious *Metatheatre*, stresses Beckett's kinship to James Joyce, it is notable that Beckett's language is not ornate or confusing on the verbal plane; the statements are perfectly clear, much like nonsense propositions in traditional logic, but they do not refer to a universe whose interconnections make sense to its participants. This is another reason why thinking is "bad" or impossible: thought requires both mental effort *and* some moral certitude that one's thoughts reflect patterns in the world out there and can have some consequences for action. Meaninglessness is most strikingly exemplified in that the characters have no consequential decisions to make. In a meaningful world the act of choice implies that something will happen one way or another, that it makes a difference which road is taken (and also if no road is taken). But here the individual gropes alone, or in concert, for he knows not what. If all thought and action are categorized as futile from the start, then meaning is absent. Life is like a phonograph needle stuck in the same groove forever. Nothing ever leads to anything else; it is a dreary rehearsal, a shadowboxing of the psyche, without plot or pilot.

All that is missing in Beckett's world, all the deprivations, afford us a dramatic simulacrum of what life is like when certain psychological and sociological imperatives are not met. But in the desolation something is left; there are survivals of human need and social organization. It is as if Beckett were telling us: you can frustrate and humiliate men, can cut them off from all that is cherished and familiar, but as long as you leave them breath they will try to act like human beings. Beckett's characters endure. They try, however feebly and grotesquely, to sustain their nerve and their relationships one to another.

Consider the effort to find meaning in the petty affairs of life, an effort like the reflex action of a mortally wounded brute. In *Godot*, when Estragon is trying on his new boots, he speaks:

ESTRAGON. We always find something, eh Didi, to give us the impression we exist?
VLADIMIR: (*impatiently*) Yes yes, we're magicians.[5]

There is communication of a sort. Verbally, it is preeminently of the type Malinowski called "phatic communion"—a symbolic linguistic activity that binds people together when they have literally "nothing to say." In these plays, nearly all the dialogue has the character of our habitual remarks of salutation, commentaries on the weather, or inquiries after the health of our respondent—that is, the words do not embody an exchange of cognitive content, a message in the strict sense, but consist rather of an emotional affirmation. The speeches recognize the person spoken to as an inhabitant of the same universe of discourse; they say, in effect, "We are human together and concerned to preserve the intercourse between us." Martin Esslin points out that language is only a part of what transpires on stage:

In the "literary" theatre, language remains the predominant component. In the anti-literary theatre of the circus or the music hall, language is reduced to a very subordinate role. The Theatre of the Absurd has regained the freedom of using language as merely one—sometimes dominant, sometimes submerged—component of its multidimensional poetic imagery. By putting the language of a scene in contrast to the action, by reducing it to meaningless patter, or by abandoning discursive logic for the poetic logic of association or assonance, the Theatre of the Absurd has opened up a new dimension of the stage.[6]

The players are human too in their occasional flashes of remembered joy, of poignant groping excursions back to a better world. These scraps of memory, indications that man is the time-binding creature Korzybski termed him, betray a striving to be human even in a world where time has dissolved. For they are inclinations, however weak, to preserve the continuity of personal identity. Their homely guise, again, stresses the human scale: the world probably does not end with a bang or a whimper but with the tranquil recollection of a summer afternoon's outing.

Humor is another residue of the daylight world. It is a bitter, cynical, self-deprecating humor that seems to serve as some defense against the full realization of horror. Or better, it is a vehicle for taunting fate: "If *this* is all you can do to me, and what could be worse, I'll laugh." Beckett's plays could stand as a text for the concept of "gallows humor," that mocking, derisive refusal to be entirely cowed by harsh circumstances. This humor has been the ancient shield of the oppressed and condemned, and in these plays we are all condemned.

At length, and most importantly, there are the continuing relationships of men in pairs. Through the tragic pairs Beckett says that if we cannot love one another at least we can need one another. Research on isolation, sensory deprivation, and mental illness seems to indicate that the essence of being human is to interact with others. In a world without meaning, one helps his fellows and finds out what he is doing here, however trivial. Vladimir speaks out an existential affirmation:

Let us not waste our time in idle discourse! (*Pause. Vehemently.*) Let us do something, while we have the chance! It is not every day that we are needed. Others would meet the case equally well, if not better. To all mankind they were addressed, those cries for help still ringing in our ears! But at this place, this moment of time, all mankind is us, whether we like it or not. Let us make the most of it, before it is too late! Let us represent worthily for once the foul brood to which a cruel fate consigned us! What do you say? (*Estragon says nothing.*) It is true that when with folded arms we weigh the pros and cons we are no less a credit to our species. The tiger bounds to the help of his congeners without the least reflexion, or else he slinks away into the depths of the thickets. But that is not the question. What are we doing here, *that* is the question. And we are blessed in this, that we happen to know the answer. Yes, in this immense confusion one thing alone is clear. We are waiting for Godot to come.[7]

Although Vladimir's speech may be mock-heroic and is grossly out of keeping with the brief, tangled style that is his wont, the significant thing is that it is spoken. There is, indeed, a curious tenderness threading the edged interaction of the forlorn pairs. The rough banter, the curse, the manifest unconcern do not entirely conceal the very human bondage these men feel.

If there are, then, these several evidences that men endure as men even in extremity, we are still left at the end in no doubt about the nature of the world Beckett perceives. The few strands of hope and comradeship are thin and fragile; experience is basically negative and depriving; it is above all a momentary affair. So Pozzo speaks:

(*Suddenly furious*) Have you not done tormenting me with your accursed time! It's abominable! When! When! One day, is that not enough for you, one day he went dumb, one day I went blind, one day we'll go deaf, one day we were born, one day we shall die, the same day, the same second, is that not enough for you? (*Calmer*) They give birth astride of a grave, the light gleams an instant, then it's night once more. (*He jerks the rope.*) On![8]

It is patent that *Waiting for Godot* and *Endgame* do not fit the mold of classical tragedy; the protagonists are not noble, are smaller than life, and the reduction in their estate is implicitly assigned to a flawed universe rather than to a flawed character. Yet the plays have the cleansing power of tragedy, the stripping bare of our fates in a phenomenological revelation of lean, driving force. They show us our inhumanity in all its angular gracelessness, but in the showing they set us free. They compel us to ponder anew, to think and feel freshly about what it means to be human and to walk among men—even in Rupert Brooke's exacting phrase, to "go proudly friended."

Beckett's drama warrants Martin Esslin's incisive conclusion: "Ultimately, a phenomenon like the Theatre of the Absurd does not reflect despair or a return to dark irrational forces but expresses modern man's endeavor to come to terms with the world in which he lives. For the dignity of man lies in his ability to face reality in all its senselessness; to accept it freely, without fear, without illusions—and to laugh at it."[9]

10

Reflections on the Sociology of Literature

I once described to the eminent literary critic Kenneth Burke my attempts to teach a course called "Literature and Society." Burke responded with the very pertinent but embarrassing question of what I, as a sociologist, could do with this enterprise that any perceptive critic couldn't do as well. I have since devoted a good deal of time to trying to answer his query, with, I confess, indifferent success. The easiest answer, perhaps, is to suggest, as Elizabeth and Tom Burns do, that the social scientist and the literary critic are fundamentally at one, that they are both critics of life and of society—or at any rate critics of what creative writers tell us about how to live a life. But the easy answer, while it has its truth, is not entirely satisfying.

The first chapter of this book, "Literature, Society, and Personality," was originally published more than twenty-five years ago. Its young author, a graduate student in sociology, contended that social scientists should pay more attention to literature as a rich source for the understanding of social relations and personality structure. He asserted that literature in its universal aspects might be a basis for comprehending the "constants" in the human condition; that in its particular aspects it might be said to express certain truths about specific societies and personalities; and most audacious of all, that literature as symbolic vehicle exerts a shaping influence, that it may actually be a force for changing individuals and societies. Now I am driven to ask whether the essays assembled here go any distance toward supporting these assertions. I think the answer must be that the sociologist's reading of literature offers rather convincing support for the first two arguments and that the third proposition concerning literature as a social influence remains essentially uninvestigated and unproved.

Although the novels and plays I have discussed were not chosen to advance any overarching thesis or even to cohere thematically to advance some central interest, several problems, several threads of analysis, are recurrent. These reiterations are partially, no doubt, reflections of my own inclinations: any analyst inevitably "reads in" to literature those features that correspond to his own abiding concerns. But I believe, too, that this emergent cluster of themes informs us about important features of writers and societies in the twentieth century.

The cardinal theme expressed by the eight major writers I have examined might be phrased as "the interrogation of life." That is, the artists of our time are, above all else, questioners, boldly asking how to live, what we owe to others and to ourselves. None of them is willing to take for granted a received set of values, a fixed model of personal identity, a traditional definition of successful conduct in the individual's repertory of social roles. Every aspect of society and personality is put up for fresh analysis and testing. Adopting a kind of conceptual and perceptual nakedness, these writers (true to the links between the child and the creator) search in sophisticated naïvety for models of human fulfillment. In a modern society shot through with the familiar but still profoundly true elements of confused values, rapid change, restlessness, and the rootlessness entailed by the loss of community, they tell us that everything about our world and ourselves is up for grabs. And each suggests, with varying degrees of explicitness, that the individual in this turbulent social environment—whose clamor and despair are often matched by exquisite inner torment in the personality—must forge for himself a way of coping, a design for competence. From the robust self-assuredness of Hemingway or the quiet religious confidence of Pasternak to the aching emptiness of Beckett's void, we are constantly alerted to man's frightening freedom to choose: he *must* choose how to conduct himself. The refusal or inability to choose consciously, as in Willy Loman or Beckett's tramps, is as much a strategy for living as the forthright deliberation of Jay Gatsby or Camus's plague doctor, Rieux.

If the artist is the one who articulates the most delicate and searing of questions, if interrogation is the underlying motif as I have suggested, can we be precise about just what is being asked? I believe we can identify a series of interwoven issues.

The first of these is at once homely and grand. It is the unending search for the self, for a defined and agreeable sense of identity. Surely this quest is a universal theme in all literature, but in our own era it is marked by a very special intensity. With the passing of traditional, static societies in the modern West the individual has been thrown much more nearly on his own to make or define himself and is much less able to rely on the definitions earlier attached to a fixed community position. So writers have consistently embarked on what Erich Heller called "The Discovery and Colonisation of Inwardness," trying to penetrate the mystery of self and to frame an identity fit for dealing with the world around them. At the end of this voyage, an end that can be only temporary, they find a fluid, shifting entity—a self that is not perhaps so much "discovered" as created from the stuff of experience. Hemingway's Jake Barnes sounds the note that is echoed by others when he reflects, "Maybe if you found out how to live in it you learned from that what it was all about."[1] The self, then, is perceived not as the solid core of the personality but more nearly as a compass that requires constant readjustment: thus Camus's conception of personality as creative struggle, or James Baldwin's sense of his protagonists as fundamentally unfinished and straining toward a precarious integrity. There is a kind of iron morality attendant on the obligation to examine the self with utter honesty. Each of the doomed figures in these novels and plays, with the possible exceptions of Meursault in *The Stranger* and Yurii Zhivago, appears doomed by a refusal to look candidly and closely at the real self. In American literature especially, we encounter a long procession of failed heroes whose failures are rooted in relentless self-deception: the Gatsbys, Lomans, and Tyrones are brothers under the skin in their deluded image of self.

Self-questioning and self-seeking are drawn as necessary, indeed inevitable. But they entail extraordinary tension, a tension that may be most directly formulated as the product of the gulf between the ideal and the actual. Heroes and heroines cherish an image of the desirable, of the self that might be. Whether this image is exalted (Zhivago as poet-healer, Tyrone as Shakespearean actor) or mundane (Willy Loman as ingratiating glad-hander, Gatsby as rich and debonair) it is constantly at war with the individual's existing, known frailties. Once again, the discrepancy between the ego ideal and the self that is has always been with us; it is not a uniquely modern concern. In our own day, however, the possibilities of self-realization are so rich and diverse and the sense of personal responsibility for the life course is so keen that the discrepancy becomes heightened and sharpened to what is for many the breaking point. What Karen Horney called "the fundamental neurosis of our time"—the straining of real self to coincide with idealized self—emerges then as more than a cluster of psychological symptoms; it emerges, in fact, as a universal accompaniment of modern consciousness.

The artist's task is construed as precisely a lifelong, un-flinching confrontation with the self. Merciless raking and prob-ing of the psychological interior, fierce exploration of identity—these are the distinguishing marks of poetic heroism. The poet alone at his work becomes the prototype of authentic, coura-geous action. So it is that in twentieth-century literature we come naturally and logically to the image of the writer as hero and to the creative act as the apotheosis of humane conduct. Pasternak and Baldwin are most overt in making the artist's role central to the novel itself, in making the writer's questioning stance a model for everyman. Yet the writer as tragic hero is also the stuff of legend in the lives of O'Neill, Fitzgerald, and emphatically, Hemingway. Beckett's adamant articulation of nonmeaning might be thought the most heroic, because the most unblinkered, ex-pression of the theme. And Camus, finally, yields the most ex-alted version of the creative man coming to terms with himself in daily devotion to lucidity, in facing his phantoms down.

If the search for self is the vehicle of inward interrogation, the search for social roles turns uncertainty and ambiguity out-ward. Clearly, the image of self is only analytically separable from the roles enacted in the social relationships of the person's love or vocation or parenthood. But the self revealed (or betrayed) in its actions toward others expands the range of questioning. Just as the individual in modern literature cannot rely on a traditional self-definition, so too he must seek afresh for his conceptions of others, must imaginatively reshape the balance of rights and duties that defines his role relationships. Writers and their protagonists grope for a realization of the self as actor, and in doing so they pose basic issues about the nature of contemporary social structure. What, they ask, are the lineaments of occupational achievement, of love's fulfillment, of that precious but fragile small group, the family? Here again the artist offers no answers: what he affords is a more alert scrutiny and the injunction to perceive our interpersonal ties clearly and honestly.

The integrity of vocational roles is a primary literary concern. In part, this theme ties in with those of self-examination and the artist as hero in that occupational attainment is viewed as possible only through fidelity to the individual's self-conception. It also, however, thrusts forward the *context* of vocational striving, the social setting that frames the hero's work. Almost nowhere in these novels and plays do we observe a person satisfying himself in a conventional institutional setting. Jake Barnes as roving journalist or Dr. Rieux as physician, as free professional, may be the sole exceptions. Otherwise the dream of success is shattered by the limitations of the occupational milieu as it exacerbates the individual's inadequacies: Gatsby's mysterious work is only a means to the end of that gorgeous life-style that may recapture Daisy; Willy Loman and James Tyrone find the taste of the American Dream bitter in their divers ways; Yurii Zhivago cannot really achieve his calling as a doctor in the dense institutional apparatus of Soviet society.

Essentially, creative writers confirm and dramatize the more abstract views of the self in its "fit" with social roles set forth by Freud in psychology and Merton in sociology. As Trilling observed, modern literature may be construed as a vast fugue elaborating on the themes of Freud's *Civilization and Its Discontents*:

In its essence literature is concerned with the self; and the particular concern of the literature of the last two centuries has been with the self in its standing quarrel with culture. We cannot mention the name of any great writer of the modern period whose work has not in some way, and usually in a passionate and explicit way, insisted on this quarrel, who has not expressed the bitterness of his discontent with civilization, who has not said that the self made greater legitimate demands than any culture could hope to satisfy. This intense conviction of the existence of the self apart from culture is, as culture well knows, its noblest and most generous achievement. At the present moment it must be thought of as a liberating idea without which our developing ideal of community is bound to defeat itself. We can speak no greater praise of Freud than to say that he placed this idea at the very center of his thought.[2]

Analogously, especially in the instance of occupational roles, literary protagonists come forth as trapped in the situation Merton analyzes and Willy Loman epitomizes—the self facing a culture whose goals and the means of reaching them are discrepant. Hence the only figures who do not founder and ultimately come unstuck in their efforts at vocational achievement are those who remove themselves from structured work settings, from fixed cultural expectations. Their occupational roles are basically self-defined and in flux; they are best represented by the artist, as in Zhivago's poetic role or Baldwin's novelist Vivaldo Moore, or by the unattached professional.

If a man's work is at issue for these writers, so too is his affection and kinship. The roles of lover, friend, husband, wife, parent, child—all these are examined, questioned, now forsaken, now despaired of. The ambiguities involved in the effort to construct a self are paralleled by those involved in the attempt to nurture a stable pattern of relationships to others. Disappointment and disenchantment are the characteristic themes of role relationships in the literary works examined here. As in the occupational sphere we discover that fulfillment occurs only in free-floating roles, cut loose from ordinary institutional moorings, so in familial and friending spheres the notable successes emerge outside of and in the interstices between conventional boundaries: thus it is with Hemingway's lovers, with the tie between Gatsby and Nick Carraway, with Zhivago and Lara, with Vivaldo and Ida Scott in Baldwin's *Another Country*. The artist tells us, in effect, that only the spontaneous pairings, the freshly designed relations that transcend society's traditional apparatus of role definition, can satisfy. Particularly in the family dramas of Miller and O'Neill, but in many other instances as well, characters enmeshed in regular role relations with "standard" expectations experience bitterness and futility. What may be the sources of this experience?

At least three primary roots suggest themselves. First, in the ambiguity and confusion inherent in society's shifting definitions of the rights and duties of role partners, individuals do not know with sureness what to expect of themselves and others in a very fluid situation. Biff Loman's plaint, "I don't know what I'm supposed to want," announces the theme clearly.[3] To demand that one either abide by an archaic code of conduct or invent a new calculus of relationships may be to demand too much. Second, the imperative to search out, to construct, to realize the self has been so urgent that it often approaches an all-consuming task. Self-absorption, perhaps akin to Durkheim's model of egoistic suicide, may so captivate the protagonist's energy and attention that he looks outward with diminished capacities for interpersonal action. Beckett's tramps and survivors are very likely at the nadir in this respect, but a host of characters in these works exhibit a similar disinclination or inabilty to attend carefully to others' needs. It is as if the rigors of the inward quest render the giving or yielding of the self problematic; the hard-won but still brittle self becomes somewhat impermeable, somewhat closed off from the universe of symbolic sharing. The mutuality and the reciprocity that underlie stable role relations are hence foreshortened. And finally, the individual's heightened anticipations of the self, the idealized image of a self that might be, are often matched by exaggerated expectations of his role partners. It has often been remarked that in modern society, with its fragmented, dissipated net of kin and community, individuals may be driven to an exclusive emotional investment in some one or very few others. The nuclear family is the prototype. So in literature the characters are stridently demanding of one another, asking that the lover, wife, husband, or child be "everything." Because no one can quite meet such demands, can quite live up to the idealized picture another cherishes of him, disillusion is virtually certain. Daisy Buchanan cannot sustain Gatsby's dream of her; the coming together of Hemingway's heroes and heroines is always a partial, transitory thing; the Tyrones and the Lomans consistently fail one another and feed on unending recrimination.

What some critics have identified as the "privatization of experience" is another prominent thread in twentieth-century letters. This is surely a concomitant of the inward journey, the discovery of selfhood; but it is also a shunning of the broad institutional arena, of the universe of civic discourse. Occupational and community organization, to say nothing of the overtly political life, are notably absent. Only in Pasternak—and to a much fainter extent in Camus—does the political structuring of individual lives find expression. Again one must concede that the artist has almost always been apolitical, if not antipolitical. His hunger for the concrete details of experience and his insistence on the free exploration of alternative modes of valuing have set him in ancient opposition to the abstractions of dense institutional life. As I noted in the discussion of Pasternak, the writer is perhaps inherently subversive in this sense, carrying on a sustained enmity with the forces that would classify and categorize men, that would distract them from the felt intimacies of the daily round. Still we can ask whether the endemic civic disillusion in the West in this last quarter of our century is not prefigured and most sharply enunciated by our creative writers. In the case of the United States, it might be argued that Watergate and Vietnam, the widespread cynicism and mistrust of political leadership, the pervasive dissatisfaction with the world of work, are all tangible indicators of what the novelist and playwright had long perceived: salvation, if it is to be found at all, will be found in the private, not the public sphere.

At the core of modern writers' observations is the "open secret" of existential thought: we are caught in the moral vacuum of a meaningless predicament. The artist's wholesale rejection of traditional models of personality, of social roles, of institutional embeddedness, may be rightly seen as bold and courageous; he is the one who is willing to face what we all know in our hearts but all flinch from. We are then presented with the paradox most sharply phrased by Camus and Beckett but implicit throughout contemporary yields of the imagination. This paradox is the stubborn fact of the creative individual's endurance, his persistence in his task despite his realization of a world now ripped by confusion, now threatening to dissolve in nothingness. Facing down his fright in the moral vacuum, the creative writer fills the vacuum with his own morality of artistic effort, the honest search and the will to form. Intellectually convinced of meaninglessness, he yet struggles to weave a temporary fabric of meaning, a meaning inherent in his generous spending of symbolic energies.

One might assert that Camus's injunction to modern man—rebellion against absurdity—is implicitly obeyed by our writers in the very act of writing itself. The artist's rebellion consists in his imposing a durable symbolic pattern on the flux of experience. If the substance of modern plays and novels is importantly concerned with a search for models of competence, for ways of coping with a hard world, so the writer exemplifies the hallmarks of competence in doing his work: the courage to explore, for the sake of the venture; the audacity to question freely; the effort to master the experienced environment; the endurance to survive in a fluid, capricious social universe and to accept the self as an unfinished process of becoming.

Notes

INTRODUCTION

1. Clifford Geertz, "Deep Play,"
p. 29.
2. Archibald MacLeish, "What is
English?" p. 100.
3. William Barrett, Time of Need,
p. 10.
4. Walker Percy, The Message in the
Bottle, p. 101.

CHAPTER 1

1. Henry A. Murray, Introduction to
Clinical Studies of Personality, by
Arthur Burton and Robert E. Harris,
p. 7.
2. Gordon W. Allport, "Personality:
A Problem for Science or a Problem
for Art?" pp. 4, 5.
3. Ibid., p. 15.
4. Milton C. Albrecht, "Psychological Motives in the Fiction of Julian
Green," p. 303.
5. Gordon W. Allport, Personality:
A Psychological Interpretation, p. 211.
6. Ibid., p. 219.

CHAPTER 2

1. Malcolm Cowley, Introduction to
The Stories of F. Scott Fitzgerald,
p. xviii.
2. Henry A. Murray, "American
Icarus."
3. Ibid., p. 639.

4. Arthur Mizener, The Far Side of
Paradise, p. 4.
5. Ibid., p. 3.
6. F. Scott Fitzgerald, This Side of
Paradise, p. 19.
7. F. Scott Fitzgerald, The Great
Gatsby, pp. 89, 159.
8. Zelda Fitzgerald, Save Me the
Waltz, p. 35.
9. F. Scott Fitzgerald, The Last
Tycoon, p. 189.
10. Ibid., p. 28.
11. Murray, "American Icarus," pp.
632–33.
12. Fitzgerald, The Last Tycoon,
p. 164.
13. Murray, "American Icarus,"
p. 633.
14. Cowley, Introduction, p. xv.
15. Murray, "American Icarus,"
p. 637.
16. Fitzgerald, Gatsby, p. 8.
17. Martha Wolfenstein and N.
Leites, Movies, p. 13.
18. Florence R. Kluckhohn, "Dominant and Substitute Profiles of Cultural
Orientations" pp. 276–93.
19. Margaret Mead, Male and
Female, p. 255.
20. Lionel Trilling, The Liberal Imagination, pp. 211–12.
21. F. Scott Fitzgerald, The Stories
of F. Scott Fitzgerald, p. 177.

22. Ibid., pp. 134–35.
23. Cowley, Introduction, p. xviii.
24. Andrew Turnbull, ed., *Scott Fitzgerald*, p. 128.

CHAPTER 3
1. William Barrett, *Time of Need*, p. 65.
2. Serge Doubrovsky, "Camus in America," p. 17.
3. Ernest Hemingway, *In Our Time*, p. 179.
4. Ernest Hemingway, *For Whom the Bell Tolls*, p. 507.
5. Roger Fry, quoted in Suzanne Langer, *Problems of Art*, p. 31.
6. Ernest Hemingway, *A Farewell to Arms*, pp. 177–78.
7. Ernest Hemingway, *The Sun Also Rises*, p. 148.
8. Ibid., p. 146.
9. Malcolm Cowley, *A Second Flowering*, p. 249.
10. George Bernard Shaw, *Selected Prose of Bernard Shaw*, p. 65.
11. Irvin D. Yalom and Marilyn Yalom, "Ernest Hemingway, A Psychiatric View," p. 494.
12. Cowley, *A Second Flowering*, pp. 231–32.

CHAPTER 4
1. Daniel Schneider, *The Psychoanalyst and the Artist*, p. 247.
2. Ibid., p. 251.
3. Ibid., p. 254.
4. Arthur Miller, *Death of a Salesman*, p. 31.
5. Robert K. Merton, *Social Theory and Social Structure*, pp. 131–60. I should here give credit to my former student David Perlmutter, who first perceived the quite astonishing parallel between Merton's scheme and action of *Death of a Salesman*.
6. Miller, *Death of a Salesman*, p. 81.
7. Merton, *Social Theory*, p. 134.
8. Ibid., p. 136.
9. Miller, *Death of a Salesman*, p. 15.
10. Ibid., p. 97.

11. Ibid., p. 16.
12. Ibid., p. 95.
13. Ibid., p. 49.
14. Ibid., p. 41.
15. Ibid., pp. 22–23.
16. Ibid., p. 85.
17. Ibid., p. 131.
18. Ibid., p. 126.
19. Ibid., pp. 56, 138, 139.

CHAPTER 5
1. Eugene O'Neill, *Long Day's Journey Into Night*, p. 9.
2. Irving Howe, *Politics and the Novel*, p. 238.
3. George Meredith, *Modern Love*, pp. 58–59.
4. O'Neill, *Long Day's Journey*, p. 87.
5. Ibid., p. 150.
6. Ibid., p. 154.
7. John Henry Raleigh, "O'Neill's *Long Day's Journey Into Night* and New England Irish-Catholicism," p. 577.
8. O'Neill, *Long Day's Journey*, p. 163.
9. Ibid., p. 162.
10. Ibid., p. 61.
11. Ibid., pp. 32, 131, 93.

CHAPTER 6
1. James Baldwin, *Go Tell It on the Mountain*, p. 163.
2. James Baldwin, *Another Country*, p. 99.
3. Ibid., pp. 61, 62.
4. Baldwin, *Go Tell It*, pp. 141, 142.
5. Ibid., pp. 20, 21.
6. Ibid., pp. 65, 66.
7. Alexander H. Leighton, *My Name is Legion*, pp. 133–87.
8. Baldwin, *Another Country*, p. 295.
9. Ibid., p. 77.
10. Ibid., p. 24.
11. Ibid., p. 148.
12. Ibid., p. 250.
13. Ibid., p. 180.
14. Ibid., p. 185.
15. Ibid., p. 305.

16. Georg Simmel, *The Sociology of Georg Simmel*, p. 409.
17. Baldwin, *Another Country,* p. 10.
18. Ibid., p. 267.
19. Ibid., p. 98.

CHAPTER 7
1. Bernard Shaw, *Selected Prose of Bernard Shaw*, pp. 661, 663–64.
2. Plato, *The Republic*, p. 477.
3. Leon Trotsky, *Literature and Revolution*, pp. 220–21.
4. Boris Pasternak, *Doctor Zhivago*, p. 338.
5. Ibid., p. 404.
6. Czeslaw Milosz, *The Captive Mind*, p. 39.
7. Pasternak, *Doctor Zhivago*, p. 184.
8. Svetlana Alliluyeva, "To Boris Leonidovich Pasternak," p. 135.
9. Hans Speier, *Social Order and the Risks of War*, p. 132.
10. Pasternak, *Doctor Zhivago*, p. 75.
11. Ibid., pp. 284–85.
12. Ibid., p. 122.
13. Alliluyeva, "To Boris Pasternak," pp. 137, 138.
14. Pasternak, *Doctor Zhivago*, p. 291.
15. Ibid., p. 251.
16. Ibid., p. 523.

CHAPTER 8
1. Albert Camus, *The Stranger*, p. 19.

2. Ibid., p. 112.
3. Camus, *The Rebel*, p. 282.
4. Ibid., p. 5.
5. Camus, *The Stranger*, p. 72.
6. Albert Camus, *The Plague*, p. 229.
7. Ibid., p. 197.
8. Ibid., p. 121, 229.
9. Ibid., p. 120.
10. Ibid., p. 278.
11. Albert Camus, *The Rebel*, p. 304.
12. Camus, *The Myth of Sisyphus*, p. 115.
13. Camus, *The Rebel*, p. 306.

CHAPTER 9
1. Samuel Beckett, *Endgame*, p. 49.
2. Ibid., p. 5.
3. Ibid., pp. 9, 49.
4. Ibid., p. 68.
5. Samuel Beckett, *Waiting for Godot*, p. 44.
6. Martin Esslin, *The Theatre of the Absurd*, p. 297.
7. Beckett, *Waiting for Godot*, p. 51.
8. Ibid., p. 57.
9. Esslin, *The Theatre of the Absurd*, p. 316.

CHAPTER 10
1. Ernest Hemingway, *The Sun Also Rises*, p. 148.
2. Lionel Trilling, *Freud and the Crisis of Our Culture*, pp. 58–59.
3. Arthur Miller, *Death of a Salesman*, p. 22.

Bibliography

Abel, Lionel. *Metatheatre*. New York: Hill and Wang, 1963.

Albrecht, Milton C. "Psychological Motives in the Fiction of Julian Green." *Journal of Personality* 16 (March 1948): 278–303.

Alliluyeva, Svetlana. "To Boris Leonidovich Pasternak." *The Atlantic Monthly* 219 (June 1967): 133–40.

Allport, Gordon W. "Personality: A Problem for Science or a Problem for Art?" *Revista de Psihologie* 1 (1938): 488–502.

_____. *Personality: A Psychological Interpretation*. New York: Henry Holt and Co., 1937.

Baldwin, James. *Another Country*. New York: Dell Publishing Co., 1963.

_____. *Go Tell It on the Mountain*. New York: Dell Publishing Co., 1965.

Barrett, William. *Time of Need*. New York: Harper and Row, 1973.

Beckett, Samuel. *Endgame*. New York: Grove Press, 1958.

_____. *Waiting for Godot*. New York: Grove Press, 1954.

Camus, Albert. *The Myth of Sisyphus*. New York: Alfred A. Knopf, 1967.

_____. *The Plague*. New York: Alfred A. Knopf, 1958.

_____. *The Rebel*. New York: Vintage Books, 1956.

_____. *The Stranger*. New York: Vintage Books, 1959.

Cowley, Malcolm. Introduction to *The Stories of F. Scott Fitzgerald*. New York: Charles Scribner's Sons, 1951.

_____. *A Second Flowering*. New York: Viking Press, 1974.

Doubrovsky, Serge. "Camus in America." In *Camus: A Collection of Critical Essays*, edited by Germaine Bree. Englewood Cliffs, N.J.: Prentice Hall, 1962.

Esslin, Martin. *The Theatre of the Absurd*. New York: Doubleday and Co., Anchor Books, 1963.

Fitzgerald, F. Scott. *The Great Gatsby*. New York: Charles Scribner's Sons, 1925.

―――. *The Last Tycoon*. New York: Charles Scribner's Sons, 1941.

―――. *The Stories of F. Scott Fitzgerald*, Edited by Malcom Cowley. New York: Charles Scribner's Sons, 1951.

―――. *This Side of Paradise*. New York: Charles Scribner's Sons, 1920.

Fitzgerald, Zelda. *Save Me the Waltz*. New York: Charles Scribner's Sons, 1932.

Geertz, Clifford. "Deep Play: Notes on the Balinese Cockfight." *Daedalus* 101 (Winter, 1972): 1–37.

Goffman, Erving. *The Presentation of Self in Everyday Life*. Garden City, N.Y.: Doubleday and Co., Anchor Books, 1959.

Hemingway, Ernest. *A Farewell to Arms*. New York: Charles Scribner's Sons, 1929.

―――. *For Whom the Bell Tolls*. New York: Charles Scribner's Sons, 1940.

―――. *In Our Time*. New York: Charles Scribner's Sons, 1925.

―――. *The Sun Also Rises*. New York: Charles Scribner's Sons, 1926.

Howe, Irving. *Politics and the Novel*. New York: Meridian Books, 1957.

Kardiner, Abram and Lionel Ovesey. *The Mark of Oppression*. Cleveland and New York: World Publishing Co., 1962.

Kluckhohn, Florence R. "Dominant and Substitute Profiles of Cultural Orientations: Their Significance for the Analysis of Social Stratification." *Social Forces* 28 (May 1950): 276–93.

Langer, Suzanne. *Problems of Art*. New York: Charles Scribner's Sons, 1957.

Leighton, Alexander H. *My Name is Legion*. New York: Basic Books, 1959.

MacLeish, Archibald. "What is English?" *Saturday Review*, December 9, 1961. Reprinted in *The Golden Age: The Saturday Review 50th Anniversary Reader*, edited by Tobin, Richard L. and S. Spencer Gein. New York: Bantam Books, 1974.

Mead, Margaret. *Male and Female*. New York: William Morrow and Co., 1949.

Meredith, George. *Modern Love*. London: Macmillan and Co., 1892.

Merton, Robert K. *Social Theory and Social Structure*. New York: Free Press, 1957.

Miller, Arthur. *Death of a Salesman*. New York: Viking Press, 1949.

Milosz, Czeslaw. *The Captive Mind*. New York: Alfred A. Knopf, 1953.

Mizener, Arthur. *The Far Side of Paradise*. Boston: Houghton Mifflin Co., 1951.

Murray, Henry A. Introduction and "American Icarus." In *Clinical Studies of Personality*, edited by Arthur Burton and Robert E. Harris. New York: Harper and Bros., 1955.

O'Neill, Eugene. *Long Day's Journey into Night*. New Haven: Yale University Press, 1956.

Pasternak, Boris. *Doctor Zhivago*. New York: Pantheon Books, 1958.

Percy, Walker. *The Message in the Bottle*. New York: Farrar, Straus and Giroux, 1975.

Plato. *The Republic*. New York: Walter J. Black, 1942.

Raleigh, John Henry. "O'Neill's *Long Day's Journey into Night* and New England Irish-Catholicism." *Partisan Review* 26 (Fall 1959): 573–92.

Schneider, Daniel. *The Psychoanalyst and the Artist*. New York: Farrar, Straus, 1950.

Shaw, George Bernard. *Selected Prose of Bernard Shaw*. Edited by Diarmuid Russell. New York: Dodd, Mead and Co., 1952.

Simmel, Georg. *The Sociology of Georg Simmel*, translated and edited by Kurt H. Wolff. Glencoe, Ill.: Free Press, 1950.

Speier, Hans. *Social Order and the Risks of War*. Cambridge, Mass.: M.I.T. Press, 1952.

Trilling, Lionel. *Freud and the Crisis of Our Culture*. Boston: Beacon Press, 1955.

_____. *The Liberal Imagination*. New York: Viking Press, 1950.

Trotsky, Leon. *Literature and Revolution*. New York: Russell and Russell. 1957.

Turnbull, Andrew, ed. *Scott Fitzgerald: Letters to His Daughter*. New York: Charles Scribner's Sons, 1963.

Turgenev, Ivan. *Fathers and Sons*. New York: Random House, 1950.

White, Robert W., ed. *The Study of Lives: Essays on Personality in*

Honor of Henry A. Murray. New York: Atherton Press, 1963.

Wolfenstein, Martha and Leites, N. *Movies: A Psychological Study.* New York: Free Press of Glencoe, 1950.

Yalom, Irvin D. and Yalom, Marilyn. ''Ernest Hemingway, A Psychiatric View.'' *Archives of General Psychiatry* 24 (June, 1971): 485–94.

Index

163

adaptation of under stress, 114–17, 131; fulfillment of in struggle, 126, 127; aim of to find way to live, 129; brutality of in Beckett, 135; endurance of, 141; as unfinished and striving in Baldwin, 147

Heroes, identification of artist with: personalities, dreams, social life, activities, and failures merged in Fitzgerald, 18–28 passim, 31, 33, 35, 36, 40; Hemingway's cultivation of heroes' image, 51–52; Tyrone family parallels O'Neill's family, 74; Edmund Tyrone and O'Neill share experiences and philosophies, 74; Baldwin's come from inward experience of blackness and homosexuality, 89–91, 103; Pasternak and Zhivago—double image of artist in repressive atmosphere, 106–9, 111–14

Hobbes, Thomas, 137

Honesty: as core of style and philosophy in Hemingway, 43, 50, 51; lack of in Willy Loman, 58, 60, 62, 65; in Baldwin's report of the human condition, 89; charge on each human being to act with, 103; of Baldwin's about blackness and homosexuality, 103; poet's thirst for, 111, 113; no illusions in Camus, 119, 127; through awareness, 133; through self-examination, 147; tension a result of, 147–48; in facing phantoms down, 148

"Honeyed muse," 106

Hope: of life to come among blacks, 93; lack of in Beckett, 139–40

Horney, Karen, 73, 148

Hostility, 89, 91, 92, 93, 137, 139, 143. See also Self, aggression against

Howe, Irving, 74

Human behavior. See Behavior

Humanity: reaffirmed by Hemingway, 46; Hemingway's conception of, 47, 55; battle for in Camus, 121; dualism in, 129; external ordeals of, 129; positive aspects of brought out in extremity, 131–32; exalted image

of in Camus, 152. See also Individual; Personality; Self

Human relationships. See Interpersonal relationships

Humor: as defense against horror in Beckett, 142

I

Ibsen, Henrik, 14, 57, 105, 106

Icarus complex: as psychological pattern, 19; themes of, 19; as exhibited in life and novels of Fitzgerald, 19, 26, 28; in romantic poetry, 20; mythic philosophy and mysticism in, 20; sexual symbolism of noted in notes for The Last Tycoon, 22; fusion of ascensionism and narcism in, 24; and fall of heroes, 24

Individual, the: linguistic environment of, 14; choices of, 15, 132; Hemingway's belief in, 17, 33, 43–44; as object and instrument, 33; need for courage in, 47; as center of own universe, 54; fidelity to self of, 55, 114–15; submerged in societal expectations, 58, 60, 65, 77–82, 90, 93, 101–3, 110–15; as valued by function, 64–65; as victim of hostile society in Baldwin, 91; consequences of racial subordination for, 91, 94–96; ultimate goal of, 98; vs. society and state, 102, 105, 107, 108, 115–16, 149–50, 152; in society, 105, 130, 146; cry for in Doctor Zhivago, 108, 112, 113; in view of poet, 113; fidelity to as highest good, 113; need of for privacy, 116; must create own rationale, 120, 125; dignity of, 120, 135, 144; reconciliation of in acceptance of death, 124; belief in by Camus, 133; creativity of, 148; as unsure of self-expectations, 151. See also Behavior, human; Personality; Self

Interpersonal relationships: at heart of art forms, 7; loyalty in, 48, 55; patterns of, 23–26, 83–84, 89; lack of tenderness and affection in, 93; thwarted by absence of self-respect

119, 120; of life, 81, 120, 121–22; ideology, 119; rebellion against, 120, 121, 153; of behavior in *The Stranger*, 121–24; of vocation, 122; overcome by finding meaning in indifferent cosmos, 125; confrontation of, 128–29; in Beckett's characters, 127, 134, 135, 140–42, 146, 148, 152. *See also* Alienation

Meredith, George, 75

Merton, Robert K., 61, 62, 63, 149; strategies of for coping with American success ethic, 63–69

Metatheatre, 140

Miller, Arthur, 57–71, 150; psychological and sociological grasp of life and family, 57; cultural goals exemplified in, 61, 70; success and failure in, 61–69

Milosz, Czeslaw, 109

Mizener, Arthur, 20, 23

Modern Love, 75

Morality: rejection of language and standards of in Hemingway, 46–47, 53; of ambition, 63; immorality of failure, 77, 82; insufficiency of in *Long Day's Journey into Night*, 81, 82; lack of standards of in Camus, 122–23; reevaluation of in *The Plague*, 126; as true perception, 127; basic questions of, 129; in honest self-examination, 147; of artistic effort, 153

Motivation, 8, 12–13, 16, 59, 122–23, 135, 138

Murder: symbolic in *Death of a Salesman*, 58–59; as ultimate act of rebellion, 123–25. *See also* Death; Suicide

Murray, Henry A., 6, 19, 20, 23, 24, 26. *See also* Icarus complex

Myth of Sisyphus, 118, 121, 126

N

Nature: mastery of in Fitzgerald, 35; confrontation of man with, 43

Nihilism. *See* Meaninglessness

1984, 74, 116

Novel, the, 5, 7, 12–13; Fitzgerald's as heroic odysseys, 33. *See also* Art(s); Literature

Novelist, xiv, 6, 43, 129, 130, 131; of "ultimate concern," xii; not inexact social scientist, 29. *See also* Artist(s); Literature

O

Oedipal theme, 8, 58, 59, 128

O'Neill, Eugene, 58, 60, 69, 72–88, 109, 148, 150; illness of, 73; as artist, 73–74; honesty of in self-interrogation, 74

Orwell, George, 8, 74, 116

Ovesey, Lionel, 91

P

Past, 75, 142

Pasternak, Boris, 43, 105–17, 146, 148, 152; compared with other authors, 105, 109, 112; died little-honored and exiled, 106; unable to accept Nobel Prize, 106; censorship of, 109; demoralization and death as result of chaotic change, 110–11; as artist, 110–11, 148; crime of withdrawal into private experience, 115

Percy, Walker, xiv

Personality, 15

Personality: approaches to in art and psychology, 6, 7; varieties of in complicated civilization, 11, common features of expressed in literature, 11–12; models of in literature, 15; cult of in *Death of a Salesman*, 67; of blacks, 91; as process and creative struggle, 118, 119, 126, 130, 132, 133, 147, 153; no assumptions about worth of in Camus, 119; as life in presence of death, 120; models and view of in Camus, 124, 126, 127, 133, 147, 152; uniqueness of, 130; as alert man fully engaged in living, 133

Philosophers, 106

Piers Plowman, 10

Plague, The, 121, 125, 126, 127, 129; as text for community under duress, 131. *See also* Extremity, reactions to

Plato, 106

Poet. *See* Art(s); Artist(s); Literature

Poetics, 58, 75

172   Index

T
Tale of Genjii, 10
Tender is the Night, 23, 24, 25, 40
This Side of Paradise, 24, 25, 27
Time of Need, xiii
Tom Jones, 10–11
Theatre of the Absurd, The, 139
Three Philosophical Poets, 14
Trilling, Lionel, 17, 37, 149
Trotsky, Leon, 107–8

U
Uncle Tom's Cabin, 11
Utopia, 11
Utopian Literature, 10–11

V
Values: of vocation, 42, 48, 50–51, 53, 54, 55, 59–60, 61, 62, 122, 125, 130; of Hemingway contrasted to modern society, 54; of modern society, 59–60, 66, 129, 146; integral to action in *Death of a Salesman*, 59, 64, 70; confusion in, 80, 128, 146; conformity to, 66; of blacks, 95; sense of rightness of, 96; monolithic

code of in totalitarianism, 107; plea for those of private and individual, 108, 115; rejection of by Camus, 119–25; nature of, 132. *See also* Existentialism
Vision, 22, 46, 48, 113
Vocation. *See* Heroes, vocational striving of

W
Waiting for Godot, 134–43 passim
War, 54
Wilbur, Richard, 56
Wilde, Oscar, 13
"Winter Dreams," 39
Wirth, Louis, 102
Wolfenstein, Martha, 30
Women, role of, 27, 53, 54, 68–69, 112, 122, 139
Writers. *See* Artist(s); Literature; Novelist

Y
Yalom, Irvin D., 52
Yalom, Marilyn, 52